John Brown

Parasitic Wealth

Or, money reform. A manifesto to the people of the United States and to the workers of the whole world

John Brown

Parasitic Wealth
Or, money reform. A manifesto to the people of the United States and to the workers of the whole world

ISBN/EAN: 9783337295769

Printed in Europe, USA, Canada, Australia, Japan

Cover: Foto ©Suzi / pixelio.de

More available books at **www.hansebooks.com**

PARASITIC WEALTH

OR

MONEY REFORM.

A Manifesto to the People of the United States and to the Workers of the Whole World.

BY

JOHN BROWN.

CHICAGO:
CHARLES H. KERR & COMPANY,
1898.

*Dedicated to the cause of Social Justice
by the Author.*

PREFACE.

As these pages go to press, there comes a message of unspeakable sadnesss bearing news of Henry George's death.

A great and good man has passed away; a staunch and intrepid champion of the wronged and oppressed has laid down his life in their service.

The world is better and purer for the life of such a man, for as long as there are leaders in our midst so fearless, so incorruptible, so outspoken, there is hope for moral regeneration, hope for self-government, hope for industrial emancipation. This man stood up for the righting of deep-seated wrongs and has labored nobly in the cause of social justice. Other shoulders must take up the burden where awearied he has left it.

It is right and fitting that this preface be the eulogy of one whose works and deeds largely inspired the writing of this book, and that it be a tribute of respect and affection, more deeply felt than duly expressed, to the memory of one who devoted his life to the betterment of mankind. And though the views of social reform herein set forth diverge widely, in some respects, from those held by Mr. George—though they differ in method, detail and application, yet in the main their object is the same—the setting aright of grievous and oppressive wrongs.

It has been the writer's duty to attack a deeply-rooted economic fallacy, and to lay bare a monstrous social crime. It requires a certain amount of courage to assail accepted beliefs never before seriously questioned, but it requires infinitely more courage to abandon old beliefs for new ones. The mind warped by the prejudices and superstitions of centuries of race training and education, becomes more or less fixed and inflexible, and well-nigh impermeable to new views and conceptions. But this is an age of research and unsparing criticism; of an uprooting of cherished ideas and opinions; of an unsettling of beliefs and convictions. Even the fundamental concepts of physical science have been put on trial for bearing false witness, and are in a fair way to be convicted by the evidence. In the interpretations of nature, we now endeavor to make the mind fit and harmonize with the phenomena, instead of distorting the facts of nature to fit our mental preconceptions and prejudices. Antiquity and "respectability" are no longer credentials of reliability nor even of veracity, and we contemplate the dogmas of authority and tradition with more distrust and suspicion than with reverence and awe.

If, therefore, the views here advanced do not accord with accepted ideas, and run counter to popular beliefs and traditions, it is no indication that they are not substantially true.

In the presentation of his ideas the author has sacrificed much detail for the sake of brevity, leaving the elaborations and amplifications for those more competent for the work. It has been his fond ambition to present a feasible and practicable scheme of social reform which should guarantee even justice to all men, and whether he has successfully accomplished his task or not, is left to the judgment of the reader.

INTRODUCTION.

A great social problem confronts us, pregnant with man's destiny, and as old as history itself. It has confronted other civilizations with visage no less sullen and foreboding. It is the question of questions, the paramount issue, beside which all other issues are trifling and unimportant. Upon its peaceful solution depends the very life and fate of our institutions, and it therefore challenges the thoughtful consideration of every good citizen who has the peace and welfare of his country at heart. The duty and responsibility of citizenship seeking the general good, is the writer's only excuse for publication.

As a layman trespassing on a domain of science of exceptional difficulty he keenly feels the responsibility of his position and conclusions, and should have wished that some one better equipped and better able had assumed it.

If the views here submitted shed a ray of hope on the miserable lot of those so grievously wronged by existing conditions,—if they contribute in the least toward an orderly and peaceful solution of a great and urgent problem, then time has not been wasted.

It is of course too much to expect that the beneficiaries of the present unjust system should agree with the deductions; indeed, so strong is the force of habit, so powerful the bias of education, and so great the inertia to change in accepted ideas, that those drilled and schooled in economic methods hoary and venerable with age and heavy with the weight of authority, will of course consider it presumptuous to even put these theories to the test of criticism.

And even if prejudices of custom and training could be removed, the falsity of present conditions exposed, and the social crime of centuries laid bare, yet as the interests of the socially benefited depend on the continuation of the present system, we should hardly expect this class to become elated over any prospective change.

But while the majority of the socially benefited will reluctantly agree with the logical conclusions even when convinced of their truth, there are some men in this class so conscientious, and so strong in the sense of honor and justice, that when converted to the views here set forth will not only cheerfully relinquish the unfair advantage society gives them over their fellow men, but will gladly aid the cause of justice and reform.

To such of the unselfish and truly noble, these pages come greeting, asking their sympathy and co-operation in the cause of humanity.

To rail at millionaires is a waste of breath. It is not only useless but senseless. The millionaire class neither individually nor collectively are responsible for our social miseries. Like the tramp and pauper, the millionaire is a natural outgrowth of social perversions—the product of a faulty civilization. It is the system and not its product that must be assailed.

Those whom our social maladjustments so cruelly oppress are naturally anxious for relief, and it will not be difficult to enlist their sympathies in the overthrow of a most pernicious and unjust social system.

But the socially benefited will not be so anxious for a change, for the righting of these wrongs implies a surrender of advantages enjoyed for ages. We can only appeal to their sense of justice and honor, and indeed to their instinct of self-preservation, for society as now organized is built on a volcano, and there is no safety for any one until its foundations rest on righteousness.

The rich and powerful could hasten social reform by active sympathy and co-operation. They can also thwart the forces of justice by obstructive measures, but they cannot stop them. Whether the socially benefited co-operate in the movement toward social equity or not, the present system is doomed and its overthrow certain. In the wake of social regeneration and readjustment, follows the downfall of privilege and despotism.

It is not the aim of the author to appeal to the passions of men, but to their reason, and if in the heat of argument, by metaphor or figure of speech he take the liberties of counsel pleading the cause of justice for the wronged and oppressed, he begs to assure his readers that no feelings against classes or individuals have prompted the writing.

Principles are more potent than denunciation, and arguments more effective than eloquence. It is upon these alone that he relies for proof of his theories.

PARASITIC WEALTH.

CHAPTER I.

That much social misery prevails even in times of comparative prosperity, no observant student will deny.

That the symptoms of suffering are periodically aggravated by widespread industrial distress, we have had nearly five years of convincing proof, and the end is not yet.

Instinctively people feel that underlying these normal and abnormal social disorders there is some great latent wrong, which if righted would make mankind whole.

The reasons assigned for these social ills are as numerous as the remedies proposed for their cure. None of the schemes, however, seem to bring us nearer to the practical solution of the problem, and the Sphinx of Fate is still busy putting the riddle to an anxious and puzzled civilization. Shall we solve it, or will it solve us?

Of course, if no organic defect can be disclosed in our present social system; if no economic condition or principle has been violated, as would appear from our text books on Political Science, then there can be no redress for our social woes and we must be content to plod along in the traditional groove and make the best of it. If the nightmare of human misery and depravity which confronts us be the natural result of a well ordered civilization, then there can be no help for it. We might as well let the mad rush go on unhindered, and if millions be trampled under foot and perish in the struggle, that is their lookout; we have the comforting theories of Political Science to fall back on to soothe the troubled conscience and relieve us of moral responsibility for the social havoc.

The social question is first of all a question of moral accountability to ourselves. Can we look our crime and pauperism in the face and without reproach of conscience say that we are not to blame?

If on a fairly honest investigation, we can establish a clean and blameless record, then there is no grievance that reform can grapple with, and there can be no social problem. If on the other hand, we discover a fundamental wrong in our Social Economics, to which this misery can be traced, then it is our moral duty to at once set about removing it, for further temporizing with such an evil is a crime.

If our grievances be real and the present social arrangements be inadequate to cope with them, then there must be some one true way, apart from the present system, in which the evil may be met, and this must be the common ground on which the present system and all other schemes of social reform can agree. There must be some economic condition or principle on which all reform forces may combine for the common good. To find this condition or principle is the aim of the writer.

Applying deductively the test of ethics to the social problem, we should consider that system of society the best, which while conceding to the individual the greatest possible personal freedom consistent with the highest welfare of society as a whole, guarantees to every member of the community an equal chance in the race of life without prejudice, an equal opportunity without favor or hindrance.

The criterion of Social Equity resolves itself, therefore, simply into "Fair-play." If we enter the arena of life on equal terms as regards natural opportunities, then all the requirements of social ethics are satisfied. We have but to exert our faculties and make the proper effort, and reward comes to us in a direct ratio of our services to society. Our reward is then a measure of our effort and ability. This is justice; more we cannot ask.

Now, with our boasted "equal rights and privileges," do our laws and economic conditions guarantee fair-play to every member of the community whatever his station in life? Are we quite sure that effort and ability are rewarded according to merit, that benefits reaped are in proportion to services rendered? If so, then the present social conditions must bear witness to such equity, and the wealth of the rich must be an equivalent of prodigious services they rendered to society, and the poverty of the poor must be an indication of utter incapacity. We judge of the tree by its fruits. If our economic conditions are right, then the distribution of wealth and income must be just. If not just, then the economic conditions cannot be right.

Let us for a moment contemplate the disparities of wealth as we see them, and take a mental inventory of the comparative commercial and industrial efficiency of those who possess colossal fortunes and those who do not.

Reliable statistics could throw much light on a dark subject, but no serious investigation has been undertaken to map out the possessions of the rich and poor, and the figures are not available. However, fairly good estimates have been independently made by different competent persons as to the distribution of wealth in the United States.

Mr. Henry Gannett in his interesting book, "The Building of a Nation," has been at some pains to obtain data for his estimates. For the classification of the rich he used Bradstreet's book of ratings and utilized the eleventh census returns as far as available in estimating the wealth of other classes.

The distribution of wealth in percentages of the total on basis of population percentages appear from his abstracts as follows:

60 00 per cent. of the population own 6 per cent. of total wealth.
37 24 " " " " 37 " " "
2 47 " " " " 25 " " "
0 28 " " " " 27 " " "
0 01 " " " " 5 " " "

On a basis of 62,600 millions of dollars of private wealth in the United States in 1890, the average wealth of these classes divided among 12,690,151 families would be:

No. of Families.	Wealth.	Averages.
7,614.091	$ 3,756,000,000	493
4,725,812	23,162,000,000	4,901
313,447	15,650,000,000	49,927
35,532	16,902,000,000	475,684
1,269	3,130,000,000	2,466,510
12,690,151	$62,600,000,000	4,933

To construct a curve of "Wealth Distribution" from the above data is a comparatively easy matter. We may safely assume that among the 7,614,091 families constituting the first group, there will be every possible gradation of holdings, from nothing at the starvation end up to $986 at the other end. The second, third, fourth and fifth groups, must without break form a continuous curve from a possession of 986 dollars up to wealth amounting probably to a hundred millions or more. Plate I. shows the development of these data into a curve. The limits of the page allow us to reach a level of $150,000. Imagination must supplement the shortcomings of the page. If the limit of aggregated wealth is one hundred and fifty millions, then we must imagine the page magnified one thousand times in order to vertically represent this high level!

The contrast between the few enormously rich and the many wretchedly poor is bewildering. But this disparity might prove nothing but prodigious capacity and productive efficiency on the one hand and utter incapacity and worthlessness at the other, unless we can show that there is a bacillus in the "body social" producing symptoms of turgescence on the one hand and atrophy on the other.

According to Mr. Gannett's estimate 350,000 families (less than 3 per cent.) own 57 per cent. of the total wealth, while 12,340,000 families own the balance of 43 per cent.

POPULATION.
Percentage divisions — each division containing 1,269,000 families

| 10 | 20 | 30 | 40 | 50 | 60 | 70 | 80 | 90 | 100 |

$100,000 Level

PLATE I.
CURVE OF WEALTH.

Page must be vertically enlarged about 1,000 times to show greatest wealth

$50,000 Level

$10,000 Level

In the "Political Science Quarterly" for December, 1893, Mr. G. K. Holmes, basing his estimates on the Eleventh Census returns, starts with the wage earning and farming class, to obtain holdings of the very rich, his method being the opposite of that of Mr. Gannett. His figures for this class when arranged appear as follows:

Families.	Per Cent.	Wealth.	Average.
1,440,000	11.35	216,000,000	150
5,159,796	40.66	2,579,898,000	500
720,618	5.68	1,142,531,550	1585
752,760	5.93	1,359,741,600	1806
1,756,440	13.84	5,309,589,600	3023
1,764,273	13.90	6,749,076,593	3825
11,593,887	91.36	17,356,837,343	

Reducing these for convenience to three items, we have:

Families.	Per Cent.	Wealth.	Average.
6,599,796	52.01	2,795,898,000	424
1,473,378	11.61	2,502,273,150	1698
3,520,713	27.74	12,058,666,193	3425
11,593,887	91.36	17,356,837,343	

It thus appears that 91 per cent. of the people own 29 per cent. of the wealth, while 9 per cent. own 71 per cent. of the wealth. Completing the above statement with the celebrated classification of 4,047 millionaires given by the New York Tribune, and arranging the remaining wealth on a basis of progression, the wealth curve would appear something like that shown on Plate II.

In his excellent book "The Present Distribution of Wealth," Dr. Chas. B. Spahr, by an independent method of research, arrives at substantially the same results as Mr. Holmes, and his figures, falling within a similar wealth curve, are valuable as corroborative evidence. Dr. Spahr estimates that one per cent. of the people own half of the wealth of the country, or as much as the remaining ninety-nine.

In the Forum for November 1889, Mr. Thos. G. Shearman gave estimates of distribution, based on the wealth of the millionaire class, and on the application of the known law of averages to such holdings, to obtain the relative wealth of the other classes. His estimates of the nation's wealth and population very closely approximate subsequent census returns. Subjoined figures are taken from his article in the New York World of June 20, 1897.

Two tables were prepared; one on the basis of the British Income Tax, and the other on the basis of tax returns from the City of Boston. On the former basis, the distribution when reduced to three great classes, is found to be as follows:

POPULATION.
Percentage divisions comprising 1,269,000 families each

PLATE II.
CURVE OF WEALTH.

$100,000 level

$50,000 level

$10,000 level

Page must be vertically enlarged about 1000 times to show highest level

Class.	Families.	Wealth.	Average.
Rich,	235,310	$43,900 millions	$186,567
Middle	1,200,000	7,500 "	6,250
Working	11,565,000	11,175 "	968

From this it would appear, that less than two per cent. of the people own seventy per cent. of the wealth of the United States.

In the table on the basis of American Tax Returns, the classification is as follows:

Families	Total Wealth.	Average Wealth.
70	$ 2,625 millions	$37,500,000
90	1,025 "	11,500,000
180	1,440 "	8,000,000
135	968 "	6,800,000
360	1,656 "	4,600,000
1755	4,036 "	2,300,000
6000	7,500 "	1,250,000
7000	4,550 "	650,000
11000	4,125 "	375,000
14000	3,220 "	230,000
16500	2,722 "	165,000
50000	5,000 "	100,000
75000	4,500 "	60,000
200000	4,000 "	20,000
1000000	3,500 "	8,500
11620000	11,215 "	
13002090	62,082 "	

The above condensed under head of three great classes becomes:

Families.	Total Wealth.	Average Wealth.
182,090	$ 43,367 millions	$238,135
1,200,000	7,500 "	6,250
11,620,000	11,215 "	968

From this table it would appear that 40,000 families own over one-half, while one-seventieth part of the population (1-4/10 per cent.) owns more than two-thirds of the country's wealth.

As the influences at work in the concentration of wealth in the United States are more potent than those in England. on account of much higher rates of interest, the estimates on basis of American tax returns should be more reliable than those on basis of British Income Tax. That these influences are constantly at work and the accummulations of wealth are becoming greater and greater there can hardly be any doubt. It is probably safe to say that 250,000 families own more than two-thirds of the United States. These 250,000 families practically dictate the government policy of the nation, control our legislatures and mould public opinion largely to suit their own class interests. The masses are mere puppets in the hands of these shrewd manipulators—mere tools to do the bidding of masters. A highly efficient and influential press largely in the service and control of these people, manufactures public sentiment to order, and schools the masses within the narrow lines of political orthodoxy and blind party allegiance.

The herd is driven shouting to the quadrennial round-up, rushing blindly where the party lash impels it into one political groove or another. It cannot go wrong, for it doesn't matter much which wins. The tariff goes up or the tariff goes down, according to which party is in control: the work of the outgoing administration is promptly undone and reversed; finances are manipulated, tariffs juggled, commerce and industry upset, and this is government—the government of the most enlightened people on earth!

On Plate III. Mr. Shearman's figures have been developed into a curve of distribution. This curve is pitched to a steeper gradient, being more sudden and pronounced than its predecessors, but while the pitch varies in degree in each, these curves all show some cumulative force or agency at work rapidly heaping up the millions into the hands of a constantly diminishing minority, whilst the vast bulk of the people seem to grow relatively poorer. They all testify to some powerful influence tending to absorb and appropriate the nation's productive output and turn it over to swell the wealth of the redundantly rich.

A class of apologists for our social perversions has been coming forward with hopeful and optimistic arguments, pursuading us, that after all, mankind is

POPULATION.

Percentage divisions comprising 1,269,000 families

| 10 | 20 | 30 | 40 | 50 | 60 | 70 | 80 | 90 | 100 |

$100,000 Level

— PLATE III. —
— CURVE OF WEALTH. —

$50,000 Level

$10,000 Level
Level of Average Wealth

To show highest wealth level, page must be enlarged vertically 1000 times.

doing fairly well; that the disparities are decreasing, and the immensely rich are becoming poorer; that the middle classes are looming up, while the "working classes" are better off than before. English statistics are quoted to show the decline of English fortunes tracing back to eras prior to the modern industrial movement. The fact is, that in England and other old countries in Europe, there has been a decline in non-productive incomes, due to gradual decline in money premium. Productive effort has settled down to a condition of industrial and commercial repose. New enterprises and undertakings have not been seeking the money function very eagerly, while money volume has been expanding and its circulation has increased by improved banking methods, thus greatly reducing competitive demand for its use. In this way "Capital" yields less profit than in countries where natural resources are not yet exploited, inventive activities are keen and industrial movement intense, all making the competition for money eager and premium rates high. Land rents have also remained stationary or declined, owing to the overflow population emigrating to new countries, thus relieving the pressure of over-population and checking any advance in rents. Thus the non-productive sources of income are not as active in accumulating fortunes as on this side of the Atlantic.

With processes and methods of production vastly improved, we should naturally expect that the very lowest stratum of society would be affected by the increased productive efficiency. But while the "working classes" have been benefited in a marked degree, aggregated wealth has not apparently relaxed its grip on the sources of its inordinate growth and the disparities do not seem to have grown less. But even if it were proved, that the differences are really growing less, it would leave the problem untouched. Why should there be injustice? While we have the industrious poor with us always, we also have the idle rich with us, drawing vast fortunes from non-productive sources.

In the "Arena" for March, 1896, Mr. Geo. B. Waldron has made an attempt to estimate the income of the people of the United States by families, on fairly conservative and reasonably reliable lines. By consolidating the first two items of his classification, the averages appear to be as follows:

Families	Average Income
53.26 per cent.	393
14.75 "	735
10.89 "	1,013
9.04 "	1,438
7.12 "	2,267
3.59 "	3,950

POPULATION IN EQUAL PERCENTAGE SUBDIVISIONS.

| 10 | 20 | 30 | 40 | 50 | 60 | 70 | 80 | 90 | 100 |

$100,000 Level

— PLATE IV. —

— CURVE OF INCOMES. —

$50,000 Level

$10,000 Level

Page must be increased vertically about 60 times to show highest income.

Families	Average Income
1.10 per cent.	8,590
.22 "	24,600
.03 "	206,325
100.00	1,075

Plate IV shows the figures developed into a curve of incomes. As in the case of the curves of wealth, it may be safely assumed that there will be all possible gradations of income from zero at the low level of despair and destitution, up to an amazing income of from six to nine millions of dollars at the end of wealth and affluence. The distribution of incomes is based on a total productive capacity of 13,641 millions of dollars per year, to be divided among 12,690,151 families, each family consisting of 4-93/100 persons, of whom 1-8/10 (1.7915) are workers. The average income per family on this basis is $1075 per year. An analysis of the figures will show that nearly 80 per cent. of the families live below this average income. The average of this 80 per cent., in a diminishing series, must therefore be just one-half of the general average, or $537.50. The balance of the 20 per cent. range from $1075 per year up to several millions. It is at this end chiefly, that bank savings are accumulated. In 1891 there were 4,533,217 depositors on the books of some 1,011 savings banks. Figuring these depositors as being the workers, and assuming that the savings were not pooled, it would appear on the basis of 1.7915 workers per family, that 2,530,000 had money deposits in banks. This is less than 20 per cent. of the whole number of families. Within certain limitations, these deposits doubtless follow the income curve. We may safely assume that fully two-thirds of these range between one dollar and one hundred dollars and average only fifty dollars. The balance will range between one hundred dollars and the bank limit. A large number of depositors no doubt maintain a multiplicity of accounts at the various banks thus fictitiously swelling the number of depositors. If these estimates are fair, something like 95 per cent. of the people derive very little or no benefit whatever from money savings as a non-productive source of income, and when it is explained that the money volume is only about one-fortieth (1/40) of the wealth volume, and that therefore interest on money represents only about one-fortieth (1/40) of the interest on other forms of "Capital" held by the very rich, it will be seen that the benefits from interest on savings among the 95 per cent. of the people amounts to practically nothing.

A dollar per day wage per worker is considered a low plane of living, but one on which people could live in comparative comfort. At one dollar per day for 300 working days in the year, a family of average number of workers could earn $537 per year, or half the average income. According to the figures given, about 40 per cent., or five million families, live below the dollar level of comfort, the average income being 50 cents per day per worker. Four millions of these live below the 80 cents per day level of comfort, averaging 40 cents per day. Three millions of these receive less than 60 cents, averaging 30 cents per day per worker. Two million live below the 40 cents per day level, and average only twenty cents per day per worker, and a million of the most wretched only average 10 cents per day per worker, unless helped out by charity. We may assume that about three per cent. of the population is at all times more or less dependent on charity. They consist of the superannuated, decrepid, crippled, and incapable,—the deaf, dumb, blind and halt—the insane, idiotic and otherwise dependent; 380,700 families would embrace this class. A liberal estimate might place the number at 500,000 families. This would leave 4,500,000 self-supporting families living on from 15 cents up to one dollar per day per worker. This level of "comfort" is based upon a period of relative industrial prosperity. What the level of "comfort" has been during the last four and a half years of hard times, we can better imagine than realize.

The same potent factor active in rolling up the millions into the hands of the few, must also operate in the distribution of incomes. The curve of income shows this in the rapid rise of the level at the end of "affluence." The curve takes the same sudden leap into space. We can follow the vertical line of exaggerated income only up to the $150,000 level. To reach six to nine millions, we must imagine the page increased vertically from forty to sixty times to show the dizzy height of wealth aggregation. In the case of the curve of wealth we imagined the page vertically increased one thousand times to show the 150 million level. These figures are amazing and we fail to grasp their real meaning. What are we to say of a system which produces such results?

When the people of the United States fully realize that the nation's wealth output is slowly but surely finding its way into the hands of a diminishing minority —that the possessors of this wealth are virtually masters of industrial production—in a word, the "owners" of the domain and its products, while the balance of mankind is a kind of incidental chattel to this wealth absorbing system of Political Economy, then we may expect an investigation into our economic methods.

We cannot be industrially enslaved and remain politically free. Great disparities in power make kings and subjects. Democracy and servitude are incompatible terms. The aggressions of wealth are a menace to free institutions and must be checked if we prize our liberty. The corrupting influence of the money power permeates society from stem to core and has struck deep into our political methods. Behold the government of a great people legislating away special privileges to Trusts, Combines and Monopolies, and the disgraceful spectacle of a hungry horde of vultures over the tariff spoils! Truth is perverted to maintain this class in power, and by the most specious and shallow reasoning the people are deluded into the belief that embarassment of commerce by tariff restrictions will improve business, that to hinder trade is to encourage it, that the Foreigner pays our taxes, that monopoly privileges to the few will enrich the many, and make us all prosperous!

What are we to think of these surprising theories, and the class that promulgates them? The handwriting is on the wall and the time of reckoning with the people is at hand.

No fair student of Political Science will honestly and conscientiously maintain that the conditions which result in such enormous disparities of well-being are of normal origin. No fair minded person will contend that such conditions can have the sanction of justice or morality, or that they may be even justified on the plea of expediency. There is a fundamental wrong somewhere. The subject matter is not new; it has been fully treated by capable and well equipped scholars. The grinding injustice of present conditions has been discussed with great eloquence and ability, but all theories and schemes of reform have been dashed and shattered on the stubborn rock of Political Science. Is the science to blame? No, but the perversion of its factors to private instead of public use is the cause of our social undoing.

CHAPTER II.

Before proceeding with the further discussion of the subject, a few words of explanation in regard to economic terms and factors will be necessary to make our meaning clear.

All wealth is the offspring of human effort exerted on the materials of the earth. All human effort, whether physical or mental, is work. If in deference to the terms used by Political Economists we call human effort in its broad sense "Labor," then Wealth is the offspring of "Land" and "Labor." Only in its expanded sense will the term "Labor" be employed.

Commerce is the exchange of the products of labor that is, of forms of wealth; and Industry is the creation of new wealth.

Primitive commerce and industry were conducted by the wasteful and unsatisfactory method of barter. They were the clumsy inefficient methods of barbarism. When money came into use, civilization was born, and money became the third factor of productive effort. Land, labor and money constitute the economic trinity. The writer is conscious of uttering a most "dangerous" economic "heresy" in proclaiming money as a prime factor of production; it marks his departure from prevailing opinions. The usual classification in our text books on Political Science, is Land, Labor and Capital, with a fourth factor sometimes added as "business ability." Business ability being a form of human effort, is simply a differential of Labor and may be ignored. The word "Capital" implies two very separate and distinct things, and is therefore the source of much confusion of thought. "Capital," in the sense of wealth is a product and not a factor. It is the offspring of Land, Labor and Money. "Capital" when used in the sense of money is a true factor of production and only in that sense can it be so understood. We are now concerned with modern methods of commerce and industry—the methods of civilization—which were made possible by the use of money alone. Money takes the place of concrete wealth in exchange and production, and becomes so efficient a means of wealth creation, that to be without it implies a return to barbarism. Concrete wealth is a mere dead product, an inert tool requiring human effort to operate it. But labor must remain idle until set free by some agent or incentive. That agent is money. Money is therefore the prime mover of industrial effort, the initiative of production, the indispensable factor of wealth creation. It is as it were the controlling valve of Industrial energy—setting the wheels of industry in motion. It is the magic switch which turns on the electric power of human effort. Wealth or Capital, is the machinery through which the energy set free by the money function operates to produce more wealth; it is the dead tool of productive effort. All wealth which conduces to comfort and shelter, all improvements which assist commerce and industry and make human effort effective, are Capital. They are the tools of production. The land is our workshop and the nation's wealth the tools, and upon the elaboration and extensiveness of the plant depends the efficiency of man's effort.

Can we carry on the business of civilization by means of goods? No, it would reduce us to the dull, sluggish methods of barter, and death and famine would overtake us—civilization would perish.

Is it British wealth we want when we desire to develop our resources or build railroads? No, we do not need the wealth, for at this moment we are the richest nation on the face of the globe. We need the money.

Is it the landed or personal wealth of our American "Capitalist" we need to set going the wheels of industry? No, it is the money he can exchange for these properties. That and nothing else.

Money is one of the industrial opportunities of man, and the most efficient tool at his command. So important is the money function that we could afford to sacrifice more than half our labor rather than do without it. Indeed so essential is it, that for centuries money was considered the only true wealth of a nation, and that idea has survived to this day as the "balance of trade" fallacy—a very excusable error. Like an invention of great utility, money multiplies the effectiveness of labor many fold. To create wealth without the aid of money is to produce it under conditions of greatest disadvantage. The money function confers on productive effort an efficiency unassisted labor does not possess, so that properly speaking wealth may be said to be the offspring of Labor and the money function. These two factors of production are always associated together and cannot be separated without causing immediate industrial collapse. It thus appears that money is indispensable to production, and if in any way it may be made artificially scarce, and its function be monopolized, then premium must emerge as the price of its limitation. Such premium, though pressing heavily on productive effort, would not, if confined simply to money, affect us seriously, were it not that "money use" confers on "property use" the same prerogative of premium, and when we fully realize that the wealth volume capable of bearing premium. is about forty times that of the money of circulation, we will better appreciate the enormous proportions such a premium charge will assume.

As without the money function wealth cannot be reproduced except under conditions of greatest disadvantage, it is quite natural that if money bear a premium, all wealth. the product of money's magic power, should also bear a premium. Were this not so, then the owners of money would not part with it except in usury, and its conversion into any sort of permanent investment would be undesirable. which is absurd. It follows, therefore, that whatever interest money brings for its hire. property, the offspring of its function. must also bring for its use. It should be noted, that all wealth, the product of human effort. is perishable. and will become less valuable with advancing time. Why should it bear interest when it has a depreciating value? Money. however, is not perishable. Honest money will purchase the same equivalent of labor to-day that it will ten years hence. Money is the parent of modern industry. the creator of wealth. When money is at a premium. its offspring. wealth. born under the adversities of currency limitations. carries with it as the price of its parentage, similar premium tendencies. Experience shows that as premium declines on money, it straight-way declines on its products. As rent emerges from the monopoly of land, so interest emerges from the limitation of money.

These views are completely at variance with those advanced by economic writers and will be referred to again.

Money has two separate and distinct functions. It is the medium of exchange for commodities, or past services, impressed on the products of labor. This is commerce.

It is also the agent of production as setting labor free to produce new wealth. This is Industry. In both cases it becomes a measure of value, of services.

Money is either a form of wealth or representative of wealth. In either case it is simply an order on society for services rendered, for energy usefully expended, giving the possessor the power to levy on society for an equivalent in past or present services. It is a voucher of human effort expended productively, and as such, it is a sight draft on the products of industry, or an order on the world's productive effort. Money should therefore come to us merely as a reward for services rendered. If it comes to us in any other way, then we posses an order on society for productive effort for which no equivalent has been rendered. This is appropriation.

Wages and profit, or incomes under any other name, unless they be the measure of actual productive services, or services conferring benefits, must be a tribute on the productive efforts of others, and simply mean injustice—a violation of the eighth commandment.

Money in its last analysis, is a medium for the exchange of services.

"Whatever performs this function, does this money-work, is money, no matter what it is made of." (F. A. Walker. Political Economy.)

In primitive society money had to be some form of wealth *per se* in order to pass unchallenged as a medium of final payment. It took the form of coin made of metals used for personal adornment. The money of the past is still the money of the present. An improvement was made in substituting paper for metal, and holding the metal as a reserve for its redemption. This improvement led to the abuses of inflation, and caused so many panics and failures, that the good features of the system were to a large degree counterbalanced.

Excepting that the so called "precious" metals are a form of wealth *per se*, there has been no valid reason assigned why gold or silver should be used for money. There are some good reasons why they should not be so used. In the first place, if money be a form of wealth then to perform its money function this wealth must be withdrawn from its legitimate field of utility in the arts and industries, and this is a waste of its value in use, and therefore a useless waste of wealth.

Secondly, the volume of coin metal is not controllable and the output is a constant source of anxiety. Nothing short of an unlimited coinage law will maintain these metals at a uniform value and prevent the fluctuations of demand and supply, and unlimited coinage is not without grave dangers as will appear later.

Thirdly, an unlimited coinage law arbitrarily fixes a price on these money metals and confers a fictitious value upon them far in excess of cost of production for industrial purposes alone, thus further contributing to a waste of wealth.

The coinage law is simply a form of "protection" for a hoary headed "infant industry"—gold mining. Demonetize gold universally, and down goes the price of this privileged metal probably two-thirds of its artificial value. So thoroughly, however, are financiers and writers on Political Science committed to a metal basis, that doubtless any project of reform will be met in a spirit of intolerance and be opposed with stubborn resistance. And yet our financial system is the survival of a primitive civilization and is entirely inadequate to the growing needs of a high social development. The shortcomings are so glaring and the social disasters caused by present methods so wide-spread, that it should be superfluous to point them out. All our panics and hard times are directly traceable to financial derangements, mainly due to efforts at inflation or expansion of a limited and inadequate money volume. Our business depressions invariably originate in a money panic. Antecedent periods of similar business collapse recurring apparently at regular intervals, strengthen the general idea that such hard times are to be expected, and this adds to the feeling of insecurity and helpless resignation. An epidemic of fear and apprehension seizes the popular mind and all prepare for the worst. Enforced idleness stares millions in the face and retrenchment begins its fatal work. Demand for luxuries decreases and producers of these are laid off first. Loss of wages of the idle further reduces consumption of the less urgent articles and more producers are thrown out of work. These again lessen the demand for products, and so the hard times cumulatively become harder, until the rock bottom of social misery and distress has been reached. The descent to adversity is slow and deliberate. The vast and ponderous machinery of industrial production gradually slows down; to overcome the inertia of its great mass and momentum requires much time. The ascent to prosperity is no less slow; it requires fully as much time to start the ponderous machinery going again. The cycle is usually completed in four or five years according to circumstances, in which legislative interferences with trade must figure very largely.

Neither over-production nor under-consumption had anything to do with our business paralysis. The wheels of industry stopped in the midst of comparative prosperity without apparent cause. It originated in a distrust of our financial integrity and the tendency of gold to go to a premium. This precipitated a money panic causing financial stringency and undermining confidence in business. Fear and apprehension did the rest. There may have been no immediate occasion for the disastrous stoppage, a mere rumor may have started the financial scare, but once started we lacked the resources to check it, and like a frenzied panic-stricken crowd at the false alarm of fire, we rushed pell-mell to destruction leaving wreck and ruin in our wake.

What has the panic cost us?

The following figures of Bank Clearances of the United States are taken from the Bureau of Statistics, Treas. Dept. Abstract for 1896. The population estimates come from U. S. Treas. Dept. Circular No. 123. In order to eliminate the disturbing influence of the panic year, we are justified in leaving it out of our comparisons. We shall therefore compare figures for the three years prior to the panic year and the three years subsequent to the panic year. This should give us a very fair and reliable comparison.

Years	Bank Clearances	Population	Per Capita
1890	$58,845,279,505	62,622,250	
1891	57,298,737,938	63,975,000	
1892	60,883,572,438	65,520,000	
Average	$59,009,196,627	64,039,083	$921.45
1894	$45,028,496,746	68,397,000	
1895	50,975,155,046	69,878,000	
1896	51,977,799,114	71,390,000	
Average	$49,327,150,302	69,888,333	$705.80

Decrease per capita since the panic $215.65 or 23.4 per cent. According to this showing, the country's business has fallen off 23.4 per cent. since the panic of 1893. Unfortunately these figures are misleading and cannot be accepted without important qualifications which in themselves would introduce an error. Prior to May, 1892, the New York Bank Clearances contained the share sales of the Stock Exchange, which very largely swelled the returns. Since the establishment of the Stock Exchange Clearing House at that date, most of the sales have been cleared through the latter institution and have ceased to figure in the returns of Bank Clearances. It thus becomes clear that unless these share sales be eliminated from the Bank Clearings, we cannot expect to make a fair comparison between the volume of business prior and subsequent to the panic year. The correct amount of these stock sales is however not available and estimates would land us into doubt. Fortunately there is a way out of the difficulty. We can compare Bank Clearings of the nation outside of New York City. The following Bank Clearance figures are taken from the Commercial and Financial Chronicle, for January 1897, and are for clearances outside of New York City.

Years	Bank Clearances	Population	Per Capita
1890	$23,165,332,888	62,622,250	
1891	22,987,037,805	63,975,000	
1892	25,348,638,020	65,520,000	
Average	$23,833,669,571	64,039,083	$372.17
1894	$21,188,928,055	68,397,000	
1895	23,440,735,558	69,878,000	
1896	22,304,476,717	71,390,000	
Average	$22,311,380,110	69,888,333	319.24

Decrease per capita since the panic....................$52.93
   or 14.22 per cent. (about 1/7).

If these returns may be taken as a fair criterion of the country's business, and there seems to be no good reason to the contrary, then it would appear that the country has sustained a loss of one-seventh of its legitimate business since the money panic of 1893.

Can we realize what this loss means? There were employed in gainful occupations in 1890, according to census returns, 22,735,661 persons which is 36.306 per cent. of the population. Applying this percentage to the average population for 1894-95-96, there should have been employed in gainful occupations during that period an average of 25,411,398 persons. On the basis of loss to business which Bank Clearances reveal to us, 3,613,500 workers must have been thrown out of employment by virtue of the business collapse. This enforced idleness was doubtless distributed more or less over the whole field of occupations, among nine-tenths of the people, leaving less workers in absolute idleness, but more of them on the margin of a precarious subsistance. Mr. Geo. B. Waldron, whom we have already quoted, estimates the value of the nation's products for 1890 at 13,641 millions of dollars. The average advance in population for the years 1894-5 and 6 as compared with population in 1890, is about 12 per cent. On the basis of this average increase, the nation's productive output would have reached the sum of 15,275 millions. Assuming this to be a conservative estimate, we have lost yearly through enforced idleness the sum of 2,170 millions of dollars, which is a sum nearly equal to the entire money volume of the United States. On this basis, during the four years of business depression ending June, 1897, we have lost in actual production a sum more than three times as great as the cost of our civil war. The value thus lost, would duplicate and equip all the railroads in the Union. This is the price we paid for a depreciated and inflated currency. The figures are not at all fanciful; they are painfully real and quite within the truth.

Could this national disaster have been avoided? Most assuredly, yes. Our financial policy however, has lacked the resourcefulness of courage, self-reliance and independence. It bears the shop marks of incompetency and subserviency to foreign methods and influence. Perhaps the most ruinous piece of legislation ever perpetrated on a long suffering and patient people was that which discredited our United States notes, known as the Greenback issue, by not making them receivable for customs. This ill-advised measure surrendered the people into the hands of usurers, and caused all our financial troubles since that time. The nation owned in public lands and buildings several times the value of these obligations, and why it could not have pledged its credit and good faith for their redemption, is a marvel to man. By making these legal tenders a money of final payment with a stipulation for their gradual redemption and retirement within specified periods, they would have circulated on par with the best money in the world.

The demonetization of silver was another blunder which contributed to our financial undoing. With a fairly good influx of gold and silver coin under an unlimited coinage law, the green-backs could have been retired without causing any apparent hardship, and we should have had at least a reliable currency, though not a desirable system of money. Of course ultimate disaster must overtake the metal basis, for at best it is a temporary expedient, but in the meanwhile the country would have been saved incalculable loss, and in spite of the growing disparities between the rich and the poor, a tide of unexampled prosperity would have swept the nation recklessly onward, drowning in the din and roar of industrial activity the warning voice of the reformer. The quondam millionaires, having burst their chrysalis of poverty, would now emerge as billionaires not aspiring for commonplace titles, but for real kingdoms. Thus social reforms might have been successfully warded off for an indefinite time. Our business collapse, and the terrible suffering and havoc it caused could have been averted in due time by a judicious use of the aggregated wealth of these millionaires, for it was only necessary to turn some of the redundant wealth into industrial channels to inspire confidence in business and tide over the dangers of retrenchment, but they did not come to the rescue and their class interests have sustained irreparable damage in consequence. The wide-spread suffering of the masses has called attention to the crying economic evils and hastened the day of industrial emancipation.

CHAPTER III.

One of the most surprising things about our money system, is the absurdly small ratio of money volume to wealth volume. The amount of money in actual circulation in 1890, according to Treasury Department Circular No. 123 was $1,429,251,270, while the wealth of the nation exclusive of coin and bullion was $63,878,316,247, thus showing the money volume to be less than 2-1/4 per cent of the wealth volume. That is to say, if all the money in the land could be taken out of circulation and made available for immediate use, it could purchase less than 2-1/4 per cent. of the permanent wealth of the country; or in other words, if all this money were available, it might be possible to convert 2-1/4 per cent. of the nation's wealth into cash, and no more.

Fig 2 Plate V shows diagramatically the ratio of money volume to wealth volume. As nearly the whole volume of available currency must be in perpetual flux and movement to satisfy the demands of commerce and industry, it is plain, that under the present system money cannot be the permanent repository of savings, except in a limited way. The present repository of permanent savings is land, and improvements on land, and the money is simply used as an instrument of investment in these properties. In other words, we have no capitalists in the sense of "moneyed men." They are simply "propertied men" who can convert their property into a part of the available but limited stock of money. This is an important point to bear in mind, and we shall have occasion to refer to it later.

If we take the amount of Bank Clearances for 1890, and divide the same by the population of that year, we obtain the money movement per capita. The result is $940. If now we divide this sum by the per capita circulation of that year (22.82), we obtain 41 as the number of times every available dollar in the country functioned in the Clearing House either directly or indirectly. In other words, although only a small percentage of this money really passed from hand to hand, the dollars were in evidence forty-one times, or actually figured in forty-one transactions. But the Clearing House is not the medium of all business transactions. There are the dealings between employers and employes, between the people and the retailers, between the retailers and the wholesalers, between the people and the banks and all minor transactions not requiring credit paper, which would very considerably increase the actual movement of money. There are also the Stock Exchange transactions which have not been included. Probably a velocity of 75 times per year per dollar would fairly represent its working energy. Truly a wonderful activity—would that labor were in such great demand.

If we wish to drive a large quantity of water through a small pipe we apply pressure to give it velocity. If we desire to force a large quantity of electricity through a conductor of certain resistance, we increase the potential of the circuit. How can we carry on a large volume of business with a small volume of money? By increasing the velocity of its circulation. Credit paper and the clearing house are the instruments of propulsion or the money potential. The dollar must be in evidence in all these transactions, it must be available, but its circulation is done by proxy through credit paper by a method of debt cancellation. It is a system of swapping accounts where only a limited amount of currency actually changes hands. It is estimated that the dollar need circulate less than ten times to do one hundred dollars worth of money work, and some people have inferred that we may eventually dispense with money altogether. We might as well speak of dispensing with pipes and conduits to carry water, or conductors to convey electricity, as to speak of dispensing with money to carry on business.

In the Clearing House methods the limit of money propulsion has been practically reached, and we may expect but little if any further improvement in the velocity of its circulation. But we are constantly reminded by economic writers that the present money volume is ample to do the business of the country, that we need only our distributive share, to successfully carry on business and industry. The laws of demand and supply are cited to show that increase in volume will depreciate the value of an expanded money, or in other words that prices will advance as money volume expands. That decreased interest on an expanded currency is only apparent, and merely indicates a diffused premium on a diluted currency.

These are astonishing theories. It is argued that as "price is the ratio between two items, money and commodities," therefore an expanded money must raise prices. "Money—what it shall be worth will "depend, demand being fixed, upon the supply. The "cost of production of money will influence its value "only as it affects that supply." (Francis A. Walker, Quar. Jn'l. Economics, vol. 8, page 64.) This is virtually the "Quantity Theory" of money.

In the Jnl. of Pol. Econ. for March 1895, Dr. S. McLean Hardy examines this theory by the inductive method. Miss Hardy cites statistics of money volume, clearing house returns and average prices of staple commodities in the United States from 1860 to 1892 inclusive, and finds, that while money volume and clearing house transactions have increased very largely since 1860, prices have not risen, but actually fallen eight per cent.

Using Miss Hardy's figures, to obtain per capita circulation and clearances, the results are as follows:

PER CAPITA CIRCULATION AND CLEARANCES.

Date.	Circulation.	Per Cent.	Clearances.	Per Cent.
1860	$ 13.85	100	$230	100
1892	24.44	176	554	241

Multiplying the circulation into the velocity of its movement as shown in the clearing house transactions, we have:

$1.76 \times 2.41 = 4.2416$, or in round numbers 4. It thus appears, that money movement per capita was four times as great in 1892 as in 1860; or on the basis of its "clearance" movement in 1860 the money volume was in effect four times as great in 1892 as in 1860. Therefore to satisfy the requirements of the "quantity theory" of money, prices in 1892 should have been four times as high as in 1860, instead of which prices declined eight per cent. The refutation of the theory is complete, and humanity owes Miss Hardy a vote of thanks. It should be particularly noted also in this connection, that while bank rates of interest have very materially declined since 1860 on an increasing circulation, they have not fallen on a diluted currency, contrary to accepted ideas.

But why should an inductive test have become necessary to disprove this theory? That price is the ratio between money and commodities is relatively quite true, but it does not follow that the value of money is affected thereby, for its value is fixed by coinage law and is therefore a constant. Money as an exchange medium, is convertible at sight into any and all forms of commodities, or services. It is not only a standard of present value, but of deferred payments and purchases, and therefore equally potent for present as for future varied wants and requirements. These qualifications, together with its imperishability, have made money the chief object of human desire and ambition. It thus became the one article of ultimate, constant, and unlimited demand, and the ordinary rules of exchange cannot be said to apply to it in the sense they apply to goods. Goods are eager, money reluctant in exchanges. Goods are variable, money constant in value. Goods are competitive and money non-competitive under normal conditions. All commodities eagerly seek conversion into cash, and tend to overtake its available volume. Nothing short of the limit of actual cost of production stops them in their mad competition for money conversion, and thus the cost of "goods production" constantly approximates, through the laws of exchange, the cost of "money production"; the cost of "money production" being the "value constant." The demand for goods is limited, and their value depends upon the temporary supply meeting the temporary demand, but this law functions independently of, and entirely outside of money as a factor in their exchange.

Money as a factor of production, when industries and undertakings compete for its use, may become subject to the laws of supply and demand, but that it is subject to fluctuations of value in effecting exchanges of commodities, is unwarranted in fact or theory and a baseless assumption. Money is a value constant and therefore non-competitive, and how an expansion of its volume by legitimate means, should affect its value is difficult to undertand.

The error of the "Quantity Theory" is that it makes of money a sort of financial "Dr. Jekyll and

Mr. Hyde," one day performing its legitimate function as a respectable medium of exchange, and the next prowling and skulking about as a depraved, degraded commodity. No doubt our clumsy and barbaric system of metal currency and bullion is responsible for the confusion, but it must be remembered that when coin or bullion is used as money, it ceases to be a commodity, and when used as a commodity, it is no longer a money. It cannot be both at the same time.

If a money possess any virtue at all, it must be that of absolute permanence and stability of value. Lacking these qualifications, money becomes a treacherous and unreliable medium, and cannot function as a true standard of value. What gives our currency uniformity of value? Assuredly nothing but the coinage law.

Assuming an unlimited coinage law, we have two separate and distinct markets for gold; a natural market, where the metal is used in the arts and industries as a commodity, and an artificial market, where the metal is used in the mints for money.

The mint receives gold for coinage at a fixed rate of say, eighteen gold dollars per ounce. As long as gold obtains more than eighteen dollars per ounce in the natural market, it will not go to the mint for coinage; but when the natural market is glutted and bids less than eighteen dollars per ounce, then the metal goes to the mint. With an eager natural market, gold coins have a natural tendency to go to the melting pot, but with a surfeited natural market, trinkets have a tendency to go to the mint. Thus the value of the 23.22 grains of gold in the dollar is automatically and very satisfactorily regulated and maintained as between these two markets. The dollar can never go below its coinage value. The theory of depreciation as following legitimate expansion, contemplates, therefore, that although the market is equalized and normal, and gold just as scarce as before expansion, it has in some way become depreciated as compared with other commodities, and its purchasing power has become impaired! The falsity of this reasoning is apparent, and should require no refutation, and yet upon such reasoning the ethics of usury have indirectly rested for centuries.

Although the natural and coinage markets automatically maintain gold at a normal and uniform value, yet this value is largely fiat and fictitious when considered simply in relation to the natural market. We have seen that since its demonetization, silver has steadily declined in value until the metal in our Standard Silver Dollar is to-day worth less than 40 cents. But silver has not yet touched bottom. It has not yet been universally discarded, is still used as token money and lives in the hopes of rehabilitation with its former coinage privileges. Remove these sustaining hopes of recovered prestige, and the natural market will then appraise its value at its true worth. We may see it sold for 30 cents per ounce if not less. Restore its unlimited coinage privileges by an international coinage law, and what will be the result? Silver will go to par with gold at once at any arbitrary ratio; providing that the law is guaranteed unassailable permanence and stability. Make the ratio 15 to 1 and immediately thousands of worthless holes in the ground will become valuable, and the owners of mines profitably worked before re-monetization will become enormously rich; we shall reap a fresh crop of millionaires and multi-millionaires, and all for what? To dig up a lot of useless metal and convert it into money of fiat value.

But how about gold? It is the same. Even at the rate of 16 to 1 gold is probably worse puffed up than silver. The methods of gold extraction have been vastly improved within the last twenty-five years. Before me is a statement from an expert miner who has spent his lifetime in gold and silver mining, and who is the owner of valuable patents for treating gold and silver ores. He claims that, speaking in a general way, ores carrying less than twenty dollars' worth of gold per ton were unprofitable to mine twenty years ago. That ten years later, ores carrying half that amount could be profitably worked, and that now gold can be profitably extracted from ores carrying five dollars per ton, and as low as two and a half dollars per ton in an exceptional case.

Now, here is a decline in the margin of cultivation from superior to inferior soils of "four to one" in twenty years, and while these improved processes may not be generally available for all kinds of ores, the fact remains that the methods of extraction have been greatly cheapened, and that these cheapening processes have enabled us to work inferior mines profitably. It therefore must cost a great deal less to mine gold now than formerly from equally rich mines. Only by virtue of the coinage law has it been possible to maintain gold at a uniform value during all these years. The improved methods of ore treatment have simply crowded down the margin of cultivation to inferior mines, where now it costs as much to mine gold by superior methods, as it used to cost to mine it from rich mines by primitive methods. Like the price of rent, the price of gold is determined at the lowest margin of cultivation. It thus appears that the present value of gold is largely fiat and fictitious as that of silver was before its demonetization, and were gold suddenly demonetized, the fiction would be squeezed out of it at once. Revoke its privileges, and its glory will depart forever. The halo of "mysterious fascination" which it is said to possess and which holds spell-bound its numerous eager votaries and worshippers, will vanish into thin air. Its hollow pretense of "nobility" exposed, its fiction of "intrinsic" worth exploded, this "precious" fraud, degraded and humiliated, will take its place among the baser herd to be appraised there at its true worth. Its value will probably sink more rapidly than that of silver, for it is commercially less useful and valuuable. Where its depreciation will stop is difficult to predict, but it will hardly reach its former relative value of 1 to 16.

The mint value of gold is purely arbitrary and may readily be changed so as to expand or contract the money volume. Assuming that an International Agreement could absolutely guarantee the permanence and stability of a coinage law, and that by the enactment of an International Monetary Congress it were decreed, that twelve grains of fine gold should constitute a dollar all over the world, immediately the present dollar would become possessed of double its purchasing power—would do the money work of two dollars. Interest would fall and price of gold in the arts and industries would be doubled. Trinkets and jewelry would have a tendency to go to the melting pot—the demand for gold in the natural market would be greatly cut down on account of price, and nearly all the out-put of gold would go to the mint under an unlimited coinage law. The ratio of silver to gold would stand at something like 75 to 1. Worthless and inferior mines would be reopened, the tailings of exhausted mines reworked, and the owners of present productive mines would become rich beyond the dreams of avarice. Gold extraction would be stimulated to the highest efficiency, new Klondikes would be discovered by eager prospectors and the stream of gold flowing to the mints would expand the money volume at a dangerous pace. Gold mine owners would vie with the owners of protected monopolies and become the masters of the world.

But where will this metal basis ultimately land us? Is not the system fraught with the greatest peril even now? Can we foresee the day when by advanced chemical research gold may be produced at such low cost and in such large quantities as to smash all coinage agreements and send us to the limbo of general ruin and bankruptcy?

There is a well founded suspicion that most of the

60 or 70 so called chemical elements known to science are not elementary bodies at all, but are molecular in structure, and have simply defied our present analytic methods. May not some future synthesis based on a better knowledge of chemistry than we now possess, produce gold from true elements?

But aside from this possibility, there is always the risk of finding exhaustless deposits of gold to shake our confidence in the metal basis. Besides, invention follows in the wake of improvement and there is no telling how soon an enormously increased output in the ever increasing number of mines may overwhelm us with the yellow metal. Indeed, as long as the present metal basis is in force, this element of risk and uncertainty will tend to a panicky and speculative feeling, portending serious disturbances, if not commercial and industrial disaster.

CHAPTER IV.

It has been shown, that money volume and money movement have both largely increased since 1860, and statistics will bear us out that productive efficiency and material advancement have kept pace with money circulation.

We had reason to believe, that the movement of money had reached a practical limit, and that greater velocity of circulation cannot be expected. The conclusion is forced upon us that whatever advance in money efficiency is to be looked for in the future must come from an expansion of its volume. We have taxed the energies of the dollar to its utmost capacity, we have goaded and pushed it to the limits of endurance, and now we can do no more. We must either hire more dollars to relieve the arduous duties of the present overtaxed force, or we must pay more premium as population advances. The dollar is the busiest factor in our civilization. While labor is at a discount, the dollar is at a premium. While labor is idle, the dollar is overworked. While labor is starving, the dollar is piling up income. Why rush the dollar so?

We have seen that money volume as compared with wealth volume is very small, and that the onus of exchange and wealth productive function falls upon a limited number of hustling dollars. So small is the volume of dollars, that the bulk of the country's business is conducted on time paper or credit money, resulting in such a state of hopeless credit interdependence, that the failure of one business firm often involves and affects the stability of all, causing widespread panics and bankruptcies. So inadequate is the money volume that no considerable reserve fund can be kept in the public treasury without seriously impairing circulation, and in critical times business is kept on the verge of a panicky feeling lest contraction through hoarding cripple trade.

So small is the money force, that a premium has to be offered to coax the reluctant dollars into the financial harness, greatly to the disparagement of all industrial and business undertakings upon which this premium falls as a heavy tribute. This premium or interest is a symptom of money scarcity, and of abundant industries and undertakings competing for its use.

The word interest as used by financiers has two distinct meanings. The percentage charge which insures money against the risk of loss, is one form of interest, and the charge for the use or hire of money otherwise amply secured, is also called interest. All enterprises and undertakings partake of risk, that is, risk of loss of money invested. To cover such risk where money is loaned without adequate security, a rate of insurance is charged proportionate to the risk involved. This insurance goes under the name of interest. Such a charge is perfectly legitimate and justifiable. We shall not call into question the propriety of this kind of interest. What concerns us here is the premium on money amply secured, and its origin. We shall not question the propriety of the charge for banking and clerical work, and the fees and percentages for effecting loans, to cover expenses and salaries of that highly efficient and useful class, the Bankers. What we shall examine is the origin and ethical warrant of usury proper. It is to be clearly understood at the outset therefore, that the word "interest" is to be used simply in the sense of money hire and apart from any risk of loss of the principal being involved.

How does interest emerge? There are, say, one thousand business men of various abilities, all anxious to engage in some commercial or industrial undertaking. All of them need cash advances to develop their business and all can furnish securities for money loans. One hundred of these men have exceptional executive ability and business genius and sagacity, and can afford to pay as high as 20 per cent. on money advances rather than go idle. Two hundred men possess a very high order of business capacity and talent and can pay 15 per cent. rather than do without the cash. Five hundred men of good judgment and ability can pay 10 per cent. and swim, but the two hundred remaining possessing only average ability must have a five per cent. rate or go out of business.

If it require at least 700 business men to properly take care of the industries and commercial enterprises of the community and there is not quite enough money to satisfy the needs of that number, the competition for funds will be confined to the five hundred men of good judgment and ability, and as they cannot bid more than 10 per cent. premium for the money, that must be the normal rate of interest at which the limited money volume may be borrowed on adequate security. At least one hundred of the five hundred men of good judgment will be non-suited for lack of funds at 10 per cent., and the two hundred men of average ability will not be in the race at all. It is thus apparent that business has been competing for a limited volume of money. We may formulate a definition of interest as follows:

Interest or premium on money depends upon its volume and the demand made upon that volume by competing industrial and commercial undertakings. Interest on money emerges when the number of industrial and commercial undertakings requiring its use, tend to overtake its available volume. The rate of interest increases as the pressure of competition for the hire of money increases and is determined by what the least remunerative of the actually operative industries are obliged to pay and yet maintain themselves in competition with more successful rivals.

In plain language, interest emerges when an expanded volume of industrial and commercial enterprises is competing for a limited volume of money. Interest discourages the less remunerative industries and the less efficient promoters of business.

Scarcity of money occasions a premium charge for money use. Like rent of land emerging from land limitation or monopoly, so rent of money emerges from its limitation or monopoly. The rent collectors of these industrial opportunities obtain without exertion what naturally belongs to productive effort.

Here is the optimistic view of interest as taught by one of our most popular text books on Political Economy.

"Is the high rate of interest a hardship? No,

the hardship lies in the scarcity of capital. The high rate of interest becomes the active means of removing that hardship through increasing the supply of capital available to meet the demand. A high rate of interest is not an evil but the cure of an evil."

Indeed the cure never cures; the evil persists and is simply aggravated at times. The world's money volume is as it were, a limited sheet of water upon which it is proposed to float the ships of commerce and industry. The water is so shallow however, that whenever a successful enterprise is to be floated, the level must be raised artificially. As the level is raised in some financial dry-dock by the hydraulic power of Interest, it must be simultaneously depressed somewhere else. The volume of water is never sufficient to successfully float all the ships that would naturally ply the ports of trade, but only that number that can afford to have the water pumped up. Less water, more hydraulic power, less money, more interest.

Let us use another illustration: Suppose we have 150 fields to cultivate, 75 willing men to work, and only 50 hoes to cultivate with. Assume that the 150 fields have 30 overseers who rent them according to productiveness. The hoes are owned by "capitalists." Let us imagine that in some way these 50 hoes possess the marvelous efficiency of money and the fields cannot be successfully cultivated without them. What will happen?

Fields are in excess of men, but hoes are scarce. The fields will compete for hoes, and as they cannot all have the use of them, only 50 of the more productive will be able to enter the contest. Whatever the least productive of these 50 fields can afford to pay, that will be the normal hire of the hoes. In other words, hoes will go to a premium, fields and men will be at a discount. One hundred fields must remain uncultivated, and twenty-five men after destructive competition with the other fifty for work, will remain idle. Twenty field overseers must also remain idle.

Let us reverse this. Assume now that there are 500 hoes in stock, the same 150 fields and the same 75 men willing to work. What will happen?

There are now more hoes than fields and more fields than men. The competition must be for the men, and not only will all of them be employed at advanced rates, but the owners of the fields will likewise benefit by the collapsed monopoly of the hoes. Fifteen of the overseers will be employed superintending and the balance may find lucrative work as field hands if they desire. In other words, the men are at a premium and natural opportunities are a drug. Men are busy, hoes are idle and fields are idle.

This is an ideal condition of things. The natural opportunities for employment are boundless, limited by space only. Work is in overwhelming abundance everywhere, and an army of one hundred million workers, representing a population of nearly half a billion, could be continuously employed, and not half exhaust the resources of work in the United States, if the industrial opportunities, land and "capital," were not limited by monopoly. There can never be any competition for work in a normal social condition, any more than there is for air or water. The competition would be for efficient men to do it.

It is a well known economic phenomenon that when opportunities for investment are plenty, the demand for money is brisk and interest is high. Incidental to this active competition for money, labor is in greater demand and business improves. But like an air brake applied to the wheels of industry, interest slows up the speed of productive effort as the premium pressure increases. The money limit, as it were, calls a halt to industrial effort, and throws labor, seeking employment, into competition with itself, thus not only taxing it, but likewise leaving it in enforced idleness.

In over-crowded Europe, where agricultural possibilities have reached their limit, where productive efficiency and the plane of living are lower, where commercial and industrial effort is less active, the demand for the money function is not so brisk and the interest rates are not so high as in this country. Up to the fall of the year 1896, the bank rates in England were two per cent. But an era of activity set in during the spring of that year, owing to development of colonial enterprises and South African gold mining. The papers teemed with Promotor's Investment schemes, and demand for money became so brisk that interest rates, following the laws of exchange, increased, and shortly doubled in amount.

Now if the money volume were so ample that in a period of greatest possible industrial activity, five, or ten times as much money lay idle in the banks as could be used in commercial and industrial undertakings, premium could not arise to act as a deterrent to production. Money being eager for investment, by virtue of its abundance, would yield no premium, and the price of its hire would simply be the cost of bank services, as will be explained later.

Perhaps no question in Political Science has so puzzled economic writers as the question of interest, and in view of the apparent simplicity of the problem, it seems rather surprising that it has not ere this been satisfactorily answered. As if quite dominated by the powerful influence of authority and precedent, our teachers have chosen the beaten track and followed in the wake of their predecessors. They have indulged in abstruse speculations, and strained fact and fancy in the elaboration of ingenious theories to account for a very common-place phenomenon. Laymen and professionals have treated in learned books and essays of this subject and as many theories have been advanced as there have been writers to invent them.

Be it to the lasting honor and credit of the Church that for centuries she refused her moral support and sanction to the practice of usury and yielded only when it was demonstrated beyond a doubt that legislative restrictions actually worked hardship and retarded social development, and that it was better to tolerate the apparently unavoidable evils of usury, than to stifle social progress.

In his Political Economy, the late lamented Gen. Walker says:

"For many centuries, and even within a comparatively recent period, the Christian Church proscribed the taking of interest as a moral offense, and the laws of nearly all civilized countries made it a crime, while the voice of publicists and ethical writers alike was raised against it as a wicked and pernicious practice. Whence came the general consent in denouncing that which to-day is *accepted as a right in morals, and as practically beneficial by all except a few fanatics?"*

The author is responsible for the italics. He gladly owns to being one of the few fanatics.

The philosophical conscience was not soothed, however, until some one suggested that interest, after all, was not paid on money, but on what money purchased, as if shifting the iniquities of usury on the shoulders of wealth palliated the crime of it!

John Calvin is credited with making this discovery, and since his time writers on Economics have been trying to reconcile Political Economy with this view, and endeavoring to find a plausible theory of interest on the basis of some inherent properties in wealth or in human nature.

Speaking of Aristotle's philosophical objection to usury, Gen. Walker says, in First Lessons of Political Economy, edition of 1893:

"The error lies in the assumption that interest is paid for the use of money, whereas in fact interest is paid for the use, not of money, but of capital. A man buys a house and promises to pay the price at some future time with 'interest' meanwhile. Interest upon what? Interest upon money? He has no money. The interest promised is upon capital invested in the house."

Passing by the confusion of ideas in the citation,

the reader's attention is drawn to the last sentence which virtually surrenders his case to his adversary. The loose manner of interchangeably using the word "Capital" to mean money in one sense and the products of the money function in another, has landed the writer into a verbal inconsistency. It was by the money function that the materials of the house were created. It was the money function that built the house with the materials created by the money function. It was the money invested in the house on which interest must be paid, seeing that "he has no money" to pay cash. In the last analysis all investment consists of money, and all interest is paid on the investment. We pay for the hire of the money invested, because there is a constant demand for money in other commercial and industrial undertakings which eagerly seek its function. It must be released and interest is the forfeit price of its ransom.

Again he says:

"A merchant or manufacturer buys a stock of goods and gives his note promising to pay the price 'with interest'. Not interest upon money, for money was not used in the transaction, but interest upon Capital in the form of merchandise or materials which have been entrusted to him and out of which he expects to make a profit which he is to share with the owner of the capital."

Most marvelous reasoning! Surely the goods, for which note was given have not only been the product of the money function, but in turn they have cost the wholesaler money, and he doubtless gave his note for them "with interest" to pay the manufacturer for money used productively; and the manufacturer in turn gave the bank a mortgage to secure not only the principal but the interest also. The interest is always paid on money and on nothing else. How can it be otherwise? Do what we will, we cannot get away from the money function in commerce and industry, for even barter is carried on in terms of money. Money is an industrial factor and wealth is its product. We can no more escape the subtle, all-pervading influence of money in our civilization, than we can get out of the influence of the atmosphere and breathe.

When we unlearn the fallacy of the "Capital" theory of interest of John Calvin, and fully realize that the premium is paid on the money function of capital, then it will become quite clear that usury as we know it, with all its deplorable consequences, is simply the result of abnormal economic conditions and may be practically abolished.

The history of "usury" speculations forms a curious and interesting chapter in Political Economy. A summary of them is given in a late work by Von Böhm

Bawerk—(Capital and Interest—Prof. Smart's translation). It is a review of the various theories of Interest with an elaboration of one of his own, based on the "tendency in human nature to under-value the future in comparison to the present." This theory Professor John B. Clark aptly calls Interest for "vicarious waiting".

Among several others are the theories of "Land Investment," "Spontaneous Reproduction" and "Reward for Abstinence."

The first assumes that, as money invested in land brings an income, that therefore investment in any form of capital must pay an interest.

The reproductive theory assumes that as crops grow and animals breed without man's assistance, therefore it is in the nature of capital to possess like power of reproduction.

The reward for abstinence theory is expressed in Prof. Hadley's Economics, pages 268-269, as follows:

"The system of interest was approved by jurists because the accumulation and use of capital was advantageous to society as a whole and increased the public wealth." "With this end in view, society was willing to offer rewards to those who would abstain from destroying wealth and would use it productively."

The land and reproductive theories carry their own

refutation. Von Böhm Bawerk's explanation, like that of the reward for abstinence, appears plausible in theory, but is lacking in practice. They are both, speaking generally, based on personal sacrifice.

Let us examine the reward for abstinence theory.

The sacrifice of abstinence has its full measure of reward in possession. That the possession should in addition give the possessor an undue advantage over the productive effort of others is not contemplated in the reward.

Human effort tends to move in the line of least discomfort. The idea of discomfort in the normal man embraces not only the pressing needs of the present, but likewise the urgent wants of the future. This gives rise to prudence and thrift. The discomfort of present abstemiousness is fully counterbalanced by the satisfaction and comfort of providing against the distresses of future privation and penury. In the miser this instinct is abnormally developed, and in the spendthrift wholly lacking. Except in the case of the morally depraved, the motive of thrift and saving is independent of the sordid instinct our economic writers would have us believe. In other words, people do not save money for the sake of obtaining usury on it, but for the purpose of providing against sickness and old age. A high premium might act as an additional inducement for the sordid-minded to save their money; in fact, usury is doubtless responsible for much of the immorality of greed and avarice, but even then the incentive must be weak compared with the real motive of thrift.

It thus appears, that under normal and natural conditions, capital would be saved from "destruction" and accumulate without the stimulus of other than purely moral motives of thrift. Usury then, seems to have no real economic value as an inducement to saving and must simply be an incident to certain economic conditions.

The prevailing ethics of usury seemingly resolves itself into this: How can we get something for nothing?

Usury is defended on the plea that capital "snatched from the jaws of appetite" at great personal sacrifice, is a factor of industrial effort and benefits society by creating wealth. Society is willing to reward those making this sacrifice by giving them interest on this capital when used productively.

Divested of its ethical glamour, the real condition is this: By virtue of certain economic limitations, capital is enabled to unjustly appropriate a large share of the products of industry as the price of its hire.

Reward for sacrifice does not enter into the problem

at all, for barring a few exceptional cases, the suffering and sacrifice are entirely vicarious, and fall on those who make a desperate effort to save on reduced earnings. A limited few obtain control of the natural opportunities of the earth and place all productive effort under tribute. It costs them no effort or inconvenience to save—deferred hopes do not figure in patient waiting, and sacrifice of abstinence is not even thought of. The wealth rolls up of its own accord, and keeps on accumulating. It grows at the expense of the sweat and toil of those paying tribute for industrial opportunities. The suffering is vicarious. Five per cent. of the people do the saving and ninety-five per cent. do the suffering.

Another popular notion, is that Labor is under obligations to capital for its subsistence. Capital is advanced by the employer to enable Labor to subsist. Capital is a reserve fund or "grub stake," and therefore entitled to interest as the price of its use. But Labor owes capital nothing, capital has no claim whatever on Labor in that respect. Labor anticipates its reward in wages by producing wealth before being paid for it.

It is not a question whether society benefits by virtue of wealth being used productively, it is a question whether it is economically necessary to pay interest for its hire except at a negligible rate, such hire charge being an equivalent of actual services rendered.

If we can prove that under normal financial conditions, interest on money will practically cease, then we have solved the problem. What are the conditions? The answer has been plainly indicated—expand the money volume. How this can be done practically and how we can secure a currency of unchallengeable stability, will be explained further on. When will the money volume be sufficient? The money volume will be sufficient, when it is so abundant that banks will refuse to pay any premium on it—when they will charge a price for its safe-guarding. Not till then will the money volume be ample; not till then will all property cease to yield non-productive revenue and industry bear a tribute to idleness.

In his article on the "Cause of Financial Panics" in the Arena for March, 1894, Mr. J. W. Bennett writes as follows:

"The borrowed capital of the country claims more in remuneration than the country can produce. Every dollar invested in business claims a return called interest. Every dollar representing debts unpaid claims a like remuneration. There is not wealth enough to meet all these obligations and the business of the world must go into the hands of a receiver every now and then so that a new start in business may be made.

The industrial world is always in a state of potential bankruptcy, but credit tends to keep it out of the hands of a receiver."

"Any disturbance of credit precipitates a panic."

"The present wealth of the United States may be placed in round numbers at $72,000,000,000. That fully 80 per cent. of this sum pays interest may be verified by any person who cares to give the subject a thought."

"Something like 80 per cent. of the wealth of the country is in the hands of about 250,000 persons, or about one two hundred and fortieth of the population. This excludes the wealth of the well to do farmers and merchants, and it goes without saying that nine-tenths of this wealth held by the immensely rich is interest bearing. Nearly all of it is lent, or if not lent out it is invested in some business where interest on the money invested is added to the return or profits of the undertakers. The wealth in the hands of farmers and merchants is paying interest on all that is not used for the personal wants of themselves and their families, and even many of the homesteads of the country are paying interest."

"At least one-half of such wealth is interest bearing. An examination of the mortgage lists of the several States will more than bear out this estimate. We are then paying fixed charges, as the railroads put it, on about $55,000,000,000 of the country's wealth. The net rate will average about five per cent., and taking into consideration commissions and other charges, six per cent. is a low estimate of the gross rate. The interest on $55,000,000,000 at six per cent. is $3,300,000,000 per year. To get the average interest charges for the last decade, we must take the average of interest paying capital, which is about $50,000,000,000. We have then an average interest of $3,000,000,000, a sum which more than absorbs the entire yearly increase of wealth in the United States. During the last decade the wealth of this country has increased about $22,000,000,000. During the same period the interest charges were $30,000,000,000." (Mr. Bennett has since embodied his views on usury in his book, "A Breed of Barren Metal.")

Thus it seems that premium interest more than absorbs the yearly wealth increase. The cumulative power of interest will better appeal to the imagination when plotted into a curve as shown on Plate V. At ten per cent the principal is doubled every seven years, so that in less than a century the interest is sixteen thousand, three hundred and eighty-four times the principal, and after that the principal increases at such a stupendous rate that the figures soon become unmanageable. At five per cent the principal doubles every fourteen years, just half as rapidly as at ten per cent. Interest accumulates in a geometrical ratio, while savings increase arithmetically. Thus if $10 is saved up, say every seven years, in 140 years the

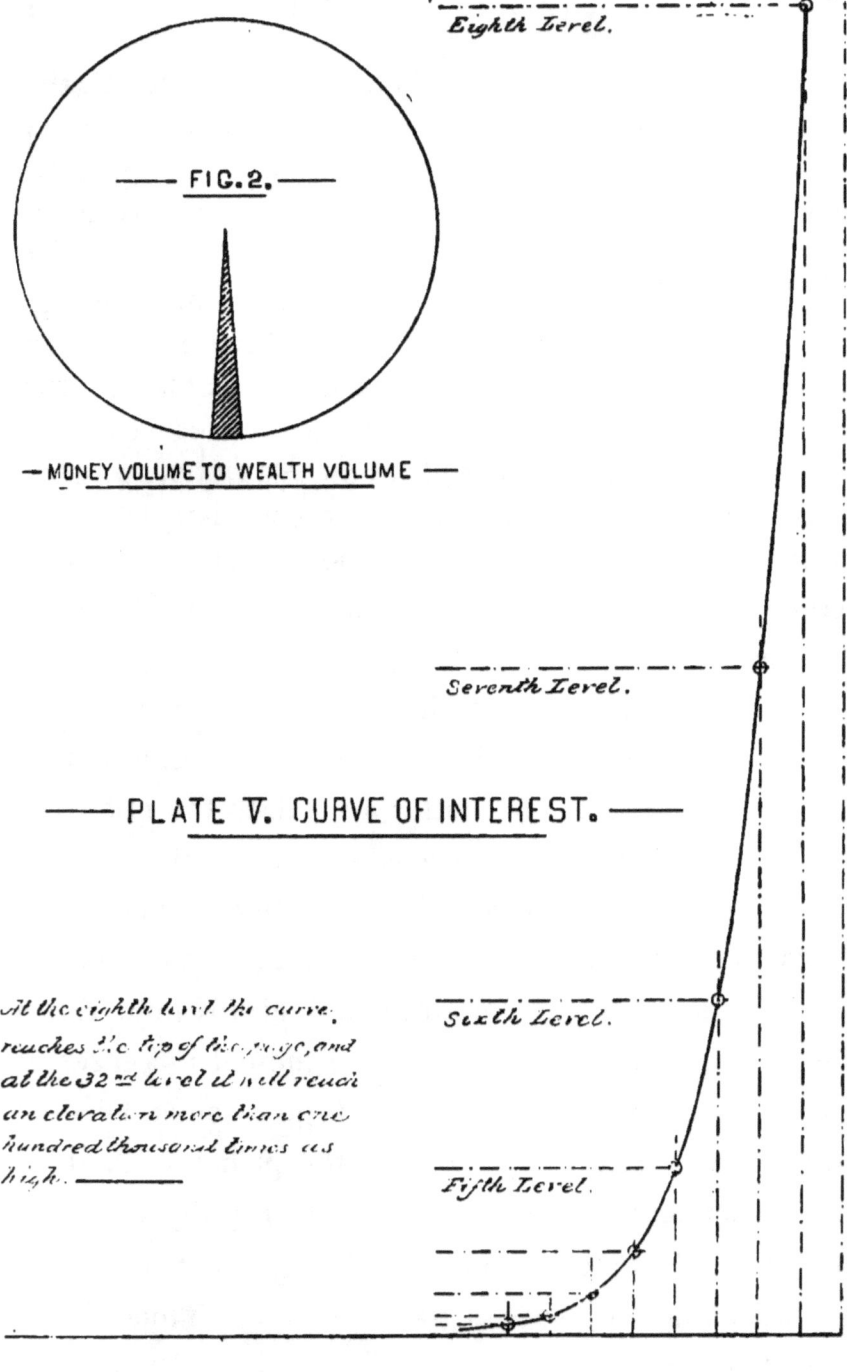

principal will amount to $200. If, however, ten dollars is put into a bank at ten per cent. interest every seven years, at the end of 140 years the principal will have become over twenty millions of dollars!

On comparing the curves of wealth with the curve of interest, the resemblance is very striking and betrays their kinship. The curves of wealth and income suddenly leap into space at the end where rent and interest absorb the nation's yearly output.

Here then is the subtle principle which makes wealth parasitic in the body of industry—the potent influence which takes from the weak and gives to the strong; which makes the rich richer and the poor poorer; which builds palaces for the idle and hovels for the diligent. This, then, is the bacillus of congested wealth—the disease germ of pauperism.

But worse than that, interest enslaves labor. We might condone the injustice of interest, if it left us free to earn, but it limits industry by closing up the avenues of employment, and fetters industrial effort by making it competitive. Employment which should be free and accessible, instead of a right, becomes a favor and a privilege! Interest is the price every industry pays capital as a license to do business. If it cannot pay the tax it must shut down. Interest is a sort of tariff on human effort to discourage enterprise;

it is a fixed charge on commerce and industry. Thus it is that we always have a glut of labor instead of a glut of employment. Think of it, even now there are millions of unemployed actually begging for work in a land of boundless opportunities and resources! Such a perverted state of things should long ago have condemned the economic conditions that produced it, and set our teachers of Political Economy to thinking. Three per cent. of the people control the avenues of employment and ninety-seven per cent. are dependent on their pleasure. And as the wealth piles up in the hands of these monopolizers of opportunities, the tribute must be heavier and escape from industrial slavery more hopeless. The wealth of the few becomes a burthen to the many—a millstone about the neck of labor—and as it grows the burthen increases. We thus realize, how that industry with its own hands forges the chains of its enslavement. And are we not reminded of it on every hand? Have we not the spectacle of lordly display and ostentation on the one hand, and abject flunkeyism on the other? Has not a perverted social condition led to perverted ideas of personal worth and respectability? Do we not see the despised "Bread Winners" treated with scorn and contempt while the idle rich are received with distinguished courtesy and respect?

The predatory class has heretofore been located in the lower strata of society; but what shall we say of the parasitic wealth on top? The social loot is not at the bottom, it is among the dizzy millions.

Where shall we place the blame for a social perversion so long endured? While instinctively all right minded people have felt that usury was morally reprehensible, and philosophic writers could find no ethical warrant for its justification—while economic writers themselves approached the subject with moral misgivings, yet all these years interest was approved as "right in morals," and land ownership (with a few honorable exceptions) justified. Symptoms of social unrest and misery counted for nothing. The perturbations and disturbances brought forth no Leverrier of Political Science to trace their cause in the economic firmament. All this time there lay at the root of our social miseries the dread germ of disease "interest," for the cultivation of which in the soil of industry, the "capital" theory of usury was and is economically responsible.

This pernicious theory has been the bane of Political Science—the evil spirit leading it from the path of economic rectitude and righteousness—and its overthrow will mark a new era in the history of a noble science, long under the shadow of doubt and suspicion as to its moral integrity.

Here is a hand sample of our present Political economy, as culled at random from a recent financial work:

"Capital is an economic quantity used for the purpose of profit."

"Whatever gives a proft is capital."

Could anything be more brutally frank and blunt than this plain statement of the case?

Let us apply this definition to land, the other factor of industry:

"Land is an economic quantity used for the purpose of profit."

"Whatever gives profit is land."

Here we have the two industrial opportunities of productive effort used as instruments of extortion for private gain, and economic writers have seen nothing wrong in a condition which permits of their limitation and monopoly. The doctrine is monstrous, and as we contemplate the enormity of it, the iniquity of the social crime grows upon us. These two great monopolies practically control the avenues of employment and place Labor entirely at the mercy of those in possession. A shrewd minority taking advantage of unjust economic conditions places the majority under tribute. Labor rendered hopelessly competitive, becomes helpless, degraded and enslaved, is sold in the open market like chattels. Can anything be more strategic? Can slavery be more absolute than under the compulsion of hunger?

The shrewd minority is in control. It is, and has been, a government of the rich, by the rich and for the rich. The masses and their interests have been a secondary consideration as we may discover by reading our text books on Political Science. The shoe pinched the poor, ignorant and down-trodden, but not the rich and clever, and therein lies the whole secret of reluctant reform. An income tax affecting the unjustly rich is promptly set aside as "unconstitutional," while a tariff tax which further depletes those already otherwise despoiled, is enforced as being just and proper. The interests of the rich are promoted by special legislation, and laws prejudicial to them set aside or not enforced.

The rich misdemeanant escapes punishment by paying a fine; the poor man unable to do so, is put in jail and his family further pauperized. The parasitic idler is shown all possible social courtesies and consideration, while the worker is socially ostracized and discriminated against. And so this precious social system of ours which creates a predatory idle class, and a despoiled productive class, simply reflects the ethical features of the economics that produced it.

All our laws seem to be framed to further encourage those socially benefited and discourage those socially wronged. The whole machinery of state, the legislative, judicial and social arrangements, all favor loot and oppress the looted.

If we examine the constituents of our legislature, we find therein, with here and there an exception, the rich and the representatives of the rich. They are either the so-called "successful" business men, or corporation lawyers whose interests are with wealth aggregations. The "successful" business man does not necessarily mean one who benefited the community as much as himself, but one who grasped the opportunities a perverted social condition offered, to become well to do at the expense of society. Naturally such people see nothing wrong in a social condition which gives them such enormous advantages over their fellowmen, and are quick to denounce those who find fault with the system, as "agitators", "demagogues", "socialists" and what not. But calling names is poor argument, and will not avail a moment against a well defined policy backed by a solid economic principle. The people are becoming very tired and impatient. They have lost confidence in the two great parties, and from sheer desperation to obtain relief, have alternately punished them by overwhelming defeats. They are tired of promises and apologies; they want reform and they will have reform.

CHAPTER V.

We have thus far confined our remarks to the money question and the evils of interest, but the solution of the money problem involves the solution of the land question. Money and Land are the two economic factors for the use of which industrial effort is taxed. Money and the products of its function take their toll in interest, and land in rent.

Thanks to the classical works of Mr. Henry George, very little if anything remains to be said on the land question that has not already been discussed with great eloquence and ability in his books.

Up to a certain point, the private ownership of land might be indifferently defended on the plea of expediency, but when immense tracts of land are monopolized for speculative purposes and rent is charged as the price of idle possession, then such forestallment becomes a question of ethics. Titles to land when traced far enough back are found in their last analyses to rest on forestallment, with possible intermediate stages of conquest or plunder, which condition of acquisition could hardly be considered valid claims to ownership.

Forty-seven years ago Mr. Herbert Spencer clearly and conclusively proved in his "Social Statics" that from the standpoint of abstract ethics, private ownership of land is not justifiable. And foreseeing the difficulties of reorganization on a basis of compensation to present owners, he says: "To justly estimate and liquidate the claims, is one of the most intricate problems society one day will have to solve."

In view of the apparent difficulties in the way of the economic realization of the abstract rights to land, Mr. Spencer had occasion later to somewhat modify his views as to the practicability or even desirability of its nationalization, seeing that in any scheme of just compensation to land owners, the interest on purchase money would probably exceed the cost of rent. Mr. Henry George has found fault with Mr. Spencer for this change of front, but when we fairly consider the reasons, we can hardly blame Mr. Spencer for believing that the lot of the dispossessed would not be improved by simply converting land rent into money rent.

Is there any wonder, in view of the doctrines of Political Science, that this master mind of the century should be puzzled over the apparent discordance between abstract ethics and practical politics, and that he should be obliged to say in his letter to the London Times:

"The reason for this state of hesitancy is, that I cannot see my way toward reconciliation of the ethical requirements with the politico-economical requirements."

Had Mr. Spencer's attention been as vitally drawn to the question of money as it had been to that of land, it is presumable he would not have been misled by the false reasoning of economic writers, and we should have had a corroborative chapter on the ethics of usury, instead of views modified to meet perverted social conditions.

A recognized principle in political ethics concedes to man the right of life, liberty and pursuit of happiness consistent with the free and unrestricted exercise of similar rights by all other men.

From this principle Mr. Spencer deduced the law that "Equity does not permit property in land." From the same principle he would have reasoned that equity does not permit the limitation by monopoly of any industrial opportunity of man, and that control or possession of such opportunities constituted an abridgment of his rights and a violation of justice.

As these opportunities are used to wrest tribute from toil, their limitation by monopoly is morally wrong. It must follow as a rule of Political Science based on equity, that incomes derived from non-productive sources are unjust.

The ultimate test of all social conditions, must be the test of abstract ethics. Unless the conditions square with rectitude and morality, they cannot be just. Let our teachers of Political Science re-examine their theories and revise their treatises. If a thing is wrong in essence, the most subtle arguments of expediency will avail not to make it right in practice. Sophistry and plausible speech will not condone a wrong.

The ethics of Political Science centers about the word "Services." All human effort, in its last analysis, is a service. Wealth in its various forms is crystallized human effort, or "past services." Creation of services and the exchange of services, is the sum total of Political Science. On the basis of such ethics, interest taking cannot be justified unless as a reward for actual services rendered. After money has been made "competitive for investment" by an expansion of its volume, "Premium" interest will cease, but a nominal residual charge of negligible but constant quantity will remain as a service charge, of which we shall speak later.

But while we can render money and therefore "Capital" premiumless, we cannot make land rentless. Land area is limited and cannot be expanded like money. It must therefore be emancipated from private control. Premiumless money and emancipated land are the watchwords, and the "Declaration of Industrial Independence," the motto of Social Reform.

Land rent seems to be nothing but interest on the purchase money, and on money invested in improvements. But it is more than that, land is a factor of production, and competition for its use like competition for the hire of money, gives rise to a "premium."

Limited money volume bears a premium—Interest.

Limited land area bears a premium—Rent.

Rent and Interest are the price society pays for limitation. They are exactly the same thing under two different names.

By the gradual expansion of the money volume and by improved methods of its circulation, interest on money declines but land cannot be expanded like money, and as population encroaches upon its available area, land premium or rent advances. If therefore, we had a premiumless money, land values would rise enormously as compared with prices of competitive products. Land being then the only non-productive source of income—the only medium where idle possession could get something for nothing—demand for its ownership would be great. The Social Problem would be only partially solved.

In any true scheme of money reform these twin

evils, interest and land ownership, must be abolished together.

The value of land increases in two ways: First by competitive demand for it, due to pressure of population, and second by public and private improvements in its vicinity. Every roadway, boulevard, railroad, canal and other transportation and business facilities, every library, art gallery, educational institution, park, public building and in fact all manner of public conveniences and improvements that make life worth living, enhance the value of land. Such increase in land values is incidental to co-operative influences, and therefore belongs to the community. All the people of the country contribute directly or indirectly to make land valuable, therefore all the people should participate in its benefits. This increased valuation is the "economic surplus" which is now appropriated by land owners to the great hurt and injury of the landless.

In this country population increases at the rate of about three per cent yearly, therefore the average land values should increase at the same rate independently of any improvements on the land, public or private. This fact largely accounts for the encouragement of immigration by the owners of land. Over-population is a curse to all but the land rich, for it enhances their wealth and places the masses under better control and subjugation to the masters of the soil.

Rent is estimated from the level of the least desirable or least productive land, called "no-rent" land. This is the level on which the "economic surplus" is drained into the pockets of land owners. As this level is forced down to less desirable lands by the pressure of advancing population, or by speculative monopoly, this "economic surplus" increases, and the drain on industry is greater. Let us not be misled by the childish arguments that rent does not affect the price of products, or the wages of labor. It is enough that it affects the purse. Rent and interest take their slice out of productive effort in a sufficiently real and tangible way. The capitalist does not feed on coin, nor does the land-lord eat soil. They both, however, take the lion's share of the nation's output.

Rent may be defined as follows:

Rent on land depends upon its available area and the demand made upon that area by competition for its use. Rent on land is the toll productive effort pays to ownership; this toll advances as demand for the soil increases, and rent, therefore, bears a definite ratio to the pressure of population. The limit to advancing rent is that limit where pressure of population trenches on the margin of subsistence.

The available land area is fast disappearing, as advancing population encroaches upon it, and land speculators obtain control.

In the Arena for September, 1896, the Rev. B. W. Williams gives some interesting figures in regard to appropriation of the public domain to private monopoly. Twenty-seven private individuals hold between them nearly twelve millions of acres of land. Fifty-six foreign corporations own more than twenty-six millions of acres of land in the United States, an area greater than the State of Indiana. With lavish extravagance and recklessness Congress deeded away over 191 millions of acres of public land to railroads and other corporations, a tract nearly as large as the combined area of France and Germany. These are astonishing facts, and show the pace at which expatriation is being accomplished.

The level of desirability is becoming lower and lower, and rents are steadily advancing. Land is the great stronghold of non-productive incomes, and in all probability the vast fortunes of the wealthy have all of them directly or indirectly been connected with land speculation and values. Speaking of the celebrated classification of millionaires published by the New York Tribune in June, 1892, Prof. Commons says in his book on the "Distribution of wealth," that taking into account the size of the fortunes, it will be found that perhaps 95 per cent. of the total value is due to investment classed as land values and natural monopolies, and industries aided by such monopolies. But as in the case of money premium, this is not its worst offense. We might overlook the exactions of rent on land and the vast fortunes made by land speculation, if it left us otherwise free to earn. But land monopoly closes up the avenues of agricultural employment to those unable to purchase land, and thus makes unemployed labor competitive and helpless.

It is a remarkable fact and one which we have already noticed, that land is probably the chief repository of savings. Land is the most desirable medium of investment, for like money and its products, it yields an income without productive exertion. It has the further advantage that as it cannot be lost, destroyed or stolen, it is therefore absolutely safe. Naturally, and by preferment therefore, land becomes the repository of savings and an instrument for drawing income from industrial effort. Our absurdly small money volume is simply a medium for effecting the conversion of one property into another and not a permanent repository of savings as it should be. If land were not purchaseable, money would either go into some useful industrial investment or remain idle as a deposit in some savings bank. Assuming the volume of money to be greatly in excess of business requirements, it would then compete for investment and bring no interest. It could be used to advantage only in productive effort and would eagerly compete for all manner of business and industrial investments where speculation and risk would give it an Insurance interest. It could be had from the banks, when amply secured, at par, with a nominal charge for bank services added. This service charge would be as a compensation for the care and responsibility of safe-guarding the money against loss, the exercise of judgment and discretion in effecting riskless loans, and all the legal, clerical and other necessary expenses connected with money transactions. Such charge for bank services would become recognized as the price of money hire. In the case of rents on dwellings and other buildings, machine plants, etc., this residual charge will probably be included as money hire. The balance of the rent will of course consist of cost of maintenance and superintendence. The use of property, causes deterioration and this waste must be covered by cost of repairs and maintenance which is a natural and just charge. Thus "rent" on Capital resolves itself into services.

Under such a money system productive effort would receive a stimulus it never had before. With land speculation closed, money would seek investment in productive undertakings and enterprises. With land rent equalized and money rent neutralized, numerous industries and undertakings would spring up that had no chance in the race before.

Labor freed from the galling yoke of industrial slavery would take fresh courage and acquire a dignity and independence it never before possessed.

CHAPTER VI.

Let us retrace our arguments:

We assumed, that if our present social conditions were right, the wealth distribution would be found to be just, but if the distribution were not just, then the conditions could not be right. We showed the curves of wealth and incomes, estimated independently by five different competent writers. We found the disparities of well-being so great as to leave no doubt in the mind that some great economic wrong lay at the root of our social miseries. We traced this wrong to the monopoly of the two great factors of production—money and land. In money, and not "capital," we identified the active factor of production, and to its limitations we traced the emergence of interest; to its derangements we traced our panics and hard times. We found that the money function conferred its premium prerogatives on its offspring wealth. We found that the "quantity theory" of money and the "capital" theory of interest misled writers as to the true nature of usury. We found that the velocity of money movement had probably reached its limit, and that no improvement in circulation could be looked for except through the expansion of the money volume to meet the demands of social and material advancement in the future. We discussed the metal basis, and found it unsuitable and unsatisfactory as a money medium, and, in fact, dangerous. We examined the ethics of usury, and found that charge for money hire had no warrant in equity, unless based on actual productive service. We examined the ethics of land ownership, and found that its limitations, like that of money, gave rise to a premium called rent; that while money could be rendered premiumless by expanding its volume, land could not be made rentless by the same means, and therefore should be emancipated from private ownership, and its benefits equalized. We concluded that any radical improvement in money reform must include land emancipation. We indulged in a speculation as to the effect on industrial production of an expanded money volume unable to take refuge in land investment.

Can we realize such conditions practically? We certainly can. Paradoxical as it may appear, out of two evils we may produce a good—out of two wrongs make a right, and all that without violating any principle of justice.

To be an ideal currency, our money must possess the following properties: it must be:

A money of final payment and uniform power in exchange.

A money of unassailable security.

A money of unchallenged value.

A money of unquestioned stability and permanence.

A money of sufficient volume to be premiumless.

What fountain source of exhaustless wealth can it be that promises such guarantees of stability and value? The answer has no doubt been anticipated. What else could it be but land?

Land value or the economic surplus in the United States may be estimated at about 30 billions of dollars. This does not of course include the value of improvements, such as structures and buildings. Nearly all of this land valuation is now in possession of private individuals and corporations. This valuation is constantly appreciating and will never have a tendency to depreciate except through race decadence. Its value, stability and permanence therefore rests on the persistence of the race itself.

Money based on land values and of ample volume cannot be "cornered" and otherwise manipulated by speculators, as our gold coin and bullion have been. It is not subject to any fluctuations of value to upset commerce and cause panics. As the source of all wealth, the value of land as a money basis stands unchallenged. It is always in evidence, always in demand, it cannot be lost, stolen or destroyed, and possesses, therefore all the desirable qualifications of a true and ideal basis of value.

How shall we emancipate this land from private ownership on principles of fair compensation, and convert it into money of circulation? Very easily indeed. The people of the United States will simply agree to pool their interests in the use of the earth. The individual owners will agree to transfer their land to the collective people of the United States on condition that the collective people issue to the individual owners receipts or certificates to the full and just value of their holdings. The United States to declare these certificates to be the constitutional money of the country—the lawful money of ultimate payment receivable for all debts, public and private. All metals heretofore used as money to be declared demonetized by law. The United States to redeem its metal currency at par in the lawful money of the land, if presented within a certain limited time, the bullion to be sold in the open market for whatever it may bring. All its paper obligations to be redeemed in the lawful money and cancelled.

We will thus at once possess a currency backed by pledges and guarantees of unchallenged value, of unassailable permanence and stability.

How shall we regulate the value of this money?

Simply by making "land value" the Standard of "exchange value"; the "Money Reform Dollar" will read about as follows:

UNITED STATES OF AMERICA.
A LIEN ON THE USE OF THE PUBLIC DOMAIN,
IN THE SUM OF ONE DOLLAR.
LEGAL TENDER FOR ALL DEBTS PUBLIC
AND PRIVATE.

The value of the dollar will be definitely fixed by its renting power. The average price of land in the United States exclusive of improvements upon it, is about $14.00 per acre. If the land yields in rent, say five per cent. net at the present price level, then one acre of average land will rent for 70 cents per year. Seven dollars of our present gold standard money will therefore rent ten acres of average land. If seven "Reform Money" dollars will likewise when presented rent ten acres of average land, then the purchasing power of the reform money will be the same as that of the present currency. The reform dollar will then purchase the same quantity of goods as the gold dollar, and their power in exchange will be equal. The value of the reform dollar will not depend so much on their number as upon their renting power, and as tax now takes the place of rent, the tax rate on land will determine exactly the value of the reform dollar. If tax rates are high, more dollars will be required to rent ten acres of land, and the dollar will buy less goods; if the tax rates are low, less dollars will be required to rent ten acres of land, and the dollar will purchase more goods. The value of the reform dollar is entirely a matter of the land tax. It may be well to state here that all taxation, save that on land, is a violation of the rights of private property. The government oversteps its true functions when it levies a toll on human effort, and it can not be justified in doing so on any grounds of equity. Land, as we have said, is man's natural opportunity, the limitation of which by private ownership works injustice and hardship on the landless. Right here is the real and true excuse for a government. The State should not only be a policeman, but the arbiter of fair play. It should not only "restrain men from injuring one another" physically and socially, but likewise industrially. In all natural and industrial opportunities the State should step in as umpire to equalize benefits, and this, in the case of land, is its only warrant for imposing a land tax. As rents cannot be abolished, the State collects them for the people and applies them for the public good. It performs the useful function of equalizing the benefits of land tenure. The same argument applies to the money question.

One of the most surprising propositions is that which advocates leaving the issue of the people's money to private enterprise. Here is a vital factor of production to be left to the vicissitudes of private speculation and profit! A most essential and important State function to be surrendered to individuals! Of course the proposition is on a par with our present theories of money and our barbaric commodity currency. Private issue and control of money is the source of great hardship and oppression to the people, but it is a boon and source of profit to individuals. Like land, money must be forever emancipated from private control and speculation.

It is entirely within the legitimate sphere of the people's government not only to issue its money, but to establish mercantile and savings banks and to transact all the riskless financial business of the country at the actual cost for banking services. As prevailing bank rates of interest determine what capital shall exact from industry for its hire, the great importance of establishing such a rate at its actual cost of bank service, becomes apparent. The people simply pool their financial issues, and resolve themselves into a "bank trust." The volume of mercantile business is constantly increasing and if healthy conditions prevailed should this year show a movement of something like 75 to 80 billions of dollars. If the banking charge for transacting this amount of business averages one tenth of one per cent., the gross yearly receipts would foot up from 75 to 80 millions of dollars, which should be far in excess of any possible expense of a very elaborate system of banking institutions. The Savings banks should receive the people's money for a small charge and guarantee absolute safety to the deposits. This money could be loaned for a very small bank service rate on proper security. It is presumable that such a rate would fall considerably below the half of one per cent. This rate would constitute a legitimate charge for legal, clerical and other bank services. All capital would claim the right to collect for such a charge, apart from its cost of maintenance and superintendence. It is of course understood that the establishment of these national institutions should carry with it no restriction on private enterprise. If private banks can serve the people better than public institutions they should be encouraged and not placed at any disadvantage.

Indeed we cannot dispense with private banks, for they will be useful where risks are involved and where speculative enterprises aid the industrial movement. Such risks of course carry with them an insurance premium. It has been explained, that "money reform" does not contemplate the discontinuance of insurance or risk premium on money or property, but a premiumless money will uniformly reduce the risk rates to the full extent of bank rates formerly charged for money hire where no risk was involved.

All money received at the peoples' banks should be destroyed, and new bills issued in its place so as to maintain the circulation clean and bright.

The issue of money is most certainly a State function. If ever there can be an urgent demand for a Government, it is to establish money, and do what private enterprise has never done and cannot do, divorce it from speculation and profit, and make it premiumless.

The State has done about everything it could do in violation of its true functions, and has left undone about everything it should do within the legitimate scope of its duty.

If the issue of money is not a legitimate function of the government then it has no legitimate function, and had better go out of business. If the issue and control of money be left to private enterprises, everything else may be left to private enterprise. The vigilance committee will protect the people, —Judge Lynch will keep order, and the other public functions will be carried on by private enterprise for private gain and profit. Individualism will run riot.

We can hardly be worse off without a government than with one continually interfering with commerce and industry by a vicious and discriminating class legislation based on a degrading paternalism. We are cursed with too much legislation and too much government. Its functions are daily growing more complex, more corrupt and more expensive. We will do well to heed the words of one of the greatest statesmen of the century:

"A wise and frugal government, which shall re-
"strain men from injuring one another; shall leave
"them otherwise free, to regulate their own pursuits
"of industry and improvements, and shall not take
"from the mouth of labor the bread it has earned;
"this is the sum of good government."

(Thomas Jefferson—First Inaugural).

It thus appears that the equalizing function of the State is its ethical warrant for the collection of the land tax and that such exercise of taxing power works in the interest of justice and prevents the spoliation of one class by the other. It further appears that the purchasing power of the Reform Dollar is simply a matter of the tax rate and under perfect control of the people. All values in exchange are thus referred to the tax rate as a standard, and whether the dollar purchases much or little of the competitive products, will depend on how much land it will rent.

If the land values in the United States amount to 30 billions of dollars, and if they have been yeilding six per cent. net income in rent, then in order that the reform dollar should maintain exactly the same purchasing power as the Standard gold dollar, the assessment should be made on the same basis. The land tax in theory would therefore yield on that basis 1800 millions of dollars per year. But practically the net yield would fall considerably below this estimate, for all land held speculatively would be at once released, and people would occupy only what they actually needed. This would set free vast tracts of valuable but unoccupied land for cultivation, and probably millions of families would now take up agricultural land at a rental who could not heretofore purchase. This would at once relieve the congested condition of the cities where rents would decline. The relief thus offered to competitive labor in the overcrowded trades and occupations would be very beneficial. Productive efficiency would be increased, and the rate of wages would therefore naturally advance.

The intelligent reader will not be apt to confound the proposed money reform with the "Real Estate Loan Association" scheme of John Law, nor will it be necessary to say that the reform money has nothing in common with the notorious French "Assignat." This absurd financial scheme was not a land emancipation reform, but a political measure for distributing confiscated church property and to replenish an exhausted treasury. The assignat was a sort of interest bearing bond, based on church real estate. With criminal recklessness these paper obligations were multiplied until they were inflated to ten times the value of the estates they represented, with the natural result—bankruptcy.

To satisfactorily and practically put the proposed Money Reform into operation will require great judgment and wisdom and much work, but once launched it will be an enduring financial reform. In order to redeem the metal coins and paper obligations of the government at their par value, the new reform money must have the same purchasing power as the gold standard, and the tax rate must therefore approximate the rent rate as closely as possible.

No discretionary powers must be given to congress in regard to the issue of money except within the limits of a well defined constitutional law. unless by consent of the people through the Referendum. The money must be issued within certain prescribed rules at a per capita rate. that rate to be constantly maintained and never exceeded. The tax rate must also be clearly defined by law on a basis of "population density" and "improvement valuation" within the district taxed.

The money may be printed and engraved by methods of such elaboration and refinement, and on special fabrics, requiring such difficult and complicated processes to reproduce that counterfeiting could not be undertaken without a most elaborate plant and very expensive appliances, leading to immediate detection.

A sudden issue of so great a volume of money as would liquidate the claims of land owners could not be undertaken without financial dissipation, and a profound disturbance of the price level. Money would seek goods on a short and unprepared market, and prices would temporarily advance very much. Goods must have time to overtake the money volume seeking them, and become competitive. All undue stimulation of trade is hurtful, and must be avoided, as it leads to eras of spasmodic prosperity, extravagance and wild speculation, and winds up in ultimate financial collapse. We here expect to accomplish by reform within a few years, what should have come to us as a natural heritage of centuries of growth and development. The financial innovation, therefore, must be introduced on the conservative lines of far sighted judgment and wisdom. The issue should take place very slowly and in small installments to maintain an economic equilibrium between a stimulated money circulation and competitive products seeking it. It should be a gradual process of some years, so that the enormous spur given to commerce and industry will not lead to reckless extravagance among the people. It should be clearly understood that an augmented money volume need not imply a greater circulation. We may have ten times as great a volume of money as at present. and circulate it only one-tenth as fast. or we may use only one-tenth of it and let the other nine-tenths remain idle.

But there is no doubt that the reform money will give industry a great impetus, increase the productive output, and correspondingly increase the consumption of goods. There will be an enlarged money circulation on an enlarged market, for all labor will be fully employed. and both the demand for the comforts of life and the supply of these comforts will be greatly augmented.

Long looked for prosperity will have come at last. and the social well-being will be without any limit except that of productive efficiency.

What will be the effect on interest of so large a volume of money?

Where we had "propertied" men, we will now have "moneyed" men, and banks will overflow with the savings of thrift. Money will now have become the repository of savings. It cannot take refuge in land investment and draw income, for speculation in land is forever closed; it must either go into improvements and buildings or other productive effort, or it must lie idle in banks. There will be more money, ten times over, than undertakings and enterprises seeking it, and consequently it will bring in no revenue. Nine-tenths of it will lie idle in banks—the dollar will have a long needed rest. Commercial banks will now require compensation from depositors for clerical and other expenses connected with money movements, and even savings banks guaranteeing absolute security to deposits would really be entitled to some nominal recompense for safe guarding the people's cash. Instead of a horde of idle money getters exacting tribute from industry by land rent and money rent, we will have men honestly earning their living in some calling useful to society. The dollar they earn will represent a dollar's worth of servies rendered. The day for getting something for nothing will have passed. Industries and business enterprises will compete with each other for capable men, and labor for the first time in the history of the world will get its just due. The farmers of the country who more than any other class have suffered from vicious tariff legislation, will benefit immensely by land emancipation. They will not only have their land but its value in money too, and their tax rates will be no more than now. The first effect of the money reform will be a general liquidation of debts and mortgages and then will follow an era of prosperity and progress never before equalled in the history of civilization. We may expect a social development exceeding the wildest dreams of reformers and a national growth and advancement equally great.

CHAPTER VII.

We lack the cohesion of race, habits and religion. We lack the bonds of a common purpose in our industrial and social life. We are an aggregation of different nationalities, heterogeneous in tastes, habits and religous beliefs, a polyglot nation, each national component striving to perpetuate its language and customs on this common soil. Our disparities make us weak and assailable as a nation—in a word we lack cohesion.

But collective ownership of the public domain will harmonize all differences and weave into the warp of our disparities the weft threads of a common interest and destiny, uniting us into a national bond of great strength and cohesion. Citizenship will acquire a new dignity, and patriotism enlarged duties and obligations. But lest we make this country a haven of refuge for the degraded and depraved of other countries—the dumping ground for European offal and refuse, we must control immigration. We must set an exalted estimate on American citizenship and hold the test of fitness to the mark. Our immigration laws must be eminently selective.

It becomes a patriotic duty—a matter of National self-preservation— that all race-degrading and deteriorating influences be kept out of the country. We have enough of our own depravity and worthlessness to take care of, and it will require a few generations to fully assimilate and elevate what raw material of native and foreign debasement and incompetency we now have in our midst. It is the duty of every nation to aspire to race supremacy, to raise its level of comfort and living to the highest possible standard, and to elevate those falling below the mark. By such race emulation and rivalry, the general well-being and happiness of mankind will be best conserved.

The criterion of material advancement is a high plane of living, and this, in fact, is a sign of productive efficiency. The test of naturalization should not only be selective as to morality, but also as to self-support. The ignorant and inefficient are an undesirable element in any community. The lower the scale of intelligence and greater the incompetency, the more numerous the breed; the higher the intelligence and ability, the fewer but more select the offspring. Reckless propagation is a menace to the continued well-being of any country. Over-population is a curse, and he is the greatest benefactor of mankind who teaches it procreative restraint, and raises its plane of living. If parental responsibility carries with it the high ideal of quality instead of quantity in offspring, trained efficiency instead of neglected education, then the millenium will be in sight. Look at India. All who have read of the horrors of plague and famine in this unfortunate land of early marriages and low plane of efficiency and living, need not wonder that some twenty millions of this criminally prolific people must die of starvation this year. Ignorance, incompetency and over population have done it. Nor will economic reform afford permanent relief to such people, for any social amelioration will at once be met and overtaken by a reckless increase in population, which nothing but the starvation limit will check.

The limit of subsistence is the lowest plane of comfort and decency on which a people will agree to live and rear families. According as people increase in intelligence and efficiency, this plane of living is raised, and consequently, in times of distress, the plane of life of such communities does not descend to the low level of starvation and disease. But these people are satisfied to live on a plane, in comparison with which our paupers are in affluence. Can we wonder then that a local famine will work so much distress?

The plane of living is the criterion of a nation's civilization, and marks the difference between a superior and an inferior race. If the nationalities of the earth were arranged into a curve of productive efficiency, it would be found that the level of comfort and plane of civilization fall within the same curve. The great problem of civilization is therefore, how to raise the standard of comfort, or more correctly speaking, to raise its productive efficiency. "Pauper" labor is worth only pauper wages because of its inferiority and inefficiency. It goes to the poor house. Under healthy economic conditions all labor has its opportunity and can get employment, but the inefficient labor though cheap, will not be sought for as eagerly as efficent labor though dear. The competition is for the best, and the more efficient will obtain the greater reward.

We have found that our average productive efficiency, taking Mr. Waldron's estimate, is about two dollars per day per worker. This efficiency is probably from twenty-five to forty per cent. higher than that of English, French or German workers, and so down the gamut of nationalities until we reach the low level of efficiency among the Chinese and Hindus.

Our level is two dollars. Why not three? The

author sees no reason why changed conditions alone should not advance our prosperity to that level within a presidential term. There is no valid reason why we cannot double our productive capacity within another decade under conditions of economic justice and fair-play.

What must be the condition of material advancement? Commercial and industrial freedom. Tariffs and meddlesome paternalism must go. Restrictions on commerce and industry must be abolished.

Two great political superstitions have dominated the mind of American workmen as the result of abnormal and perverted economic conditions. One is, that labor saving machinery and improved processes of production rob us of employment, and the other, that the so-called "Protection" by tariff tax increases employment. Nothing could be more wide of the truth. Statistics show that nearly twice as many workers per capita were engaged in the manufacturing industries in 1890 as were employed per capita in 1850, and the capital invested in these industries per capita in 1890 was nearly five times as great as in 1850, showing quite conclusively that labor saving machinery and processes have not closed the avenues of employment.

But what shall we say of that pitiful plea of national incompetency---that humiliating confession of weakness and incapacity which cries out aloud for help and "Protection?" Do the strong and capable need protection? The word should be beneath the contempt of every self respecting American who believes in manliness and self-reliance.

Protection against what? Is it against "Pauper" labor? We are importing it as fast as the steam-ship lines can carry it to these shores. It brings with it its native incompetency and degradation and fills our poor-houses and pauper institutions.

What then is the protection for? Simply to "protect" the people from buying at natural market rates what they now must purchase at monopoly rates. It is not protection but black-mail.

According to the investigations of the New York Tribune in 1892, to account for the great fortunes of the millionaire class, the statements abundantly prove that about 28 per cent. of the immensely rich obtained their wealth from protected industries. Protection means a monopoly. We have seen that the natural monopolies of Capital and Land have caused enormous disparities of wealth, but not content with these instruments of exaction, we must create a special monopoly and call it "protection," to assist the process.

The tariff is a restriction. It says to commerce and

industry: "we want less wealth." It says to human effort: "we want less efficiency."

If trade confers no benefit on man it should be stopped. If it does not increase the efficiency of human effort, it should be discontinued.

The theory of protection is the belief that by tariff restrictions we encourage the development of home industries, and that home competition is a guarantee of ultimate low prices; that by protection we encourage home labor as against foreign labor, in fact we get the better of the foreigners at every point. Ostensibly we are doing this, but in reality it works very much like the patent water-gas stove of many years ago, which was advertised to make its own gas from water, and to require no other fuel. It did make its own gas from water, but at the expense of its iron, and consumed itself chemically in the process of burning. So with these protected industries; they thrive on the national substance; they flourish at the people's expense.

Trade cannot be made one-sided; it must be reciprocal in its benefits. By trade restrictions we punish the foreigner and we punish ourselves equally. He cannot trade with us so as to get cheaply what costs him dearly to produce and give us in return cheaply what costs us dearly to produce. It hinders the exchange of benefits. It makes human effort less effective and is a loss of wealth.

When it once becomes clear to the American workman that legislative restrictions can add nothing to our wealth, but that they can and do divert money from pockets where it belongs into pockets where it does not belong; when he understands that tariff laws divert labor from natural and productive channels into artificial and unproductive channels, and that they make continued employment contingent on these artificial props, which when removed throw labor out of work, then perhaps he will no longer listen to the seductive arguments of the monopolist.

Like interest on capital and the land monopoly, these restrictions on trade exact a tribute from industrial effort. They close up the avenues of employment, make labor competitive, and place it at the mercy of the monopolist.

Make money premium-less, emancipate land, and abolish all trade restrictions and you open up three great avenues of employment now guarded by monopoly. When these are thrown open, labor will be emancipated from industrial slavery. Work—endless, infinite work—will be a drug competing for men to do it. We will then be as anxious for the foreigner to do it, as we are now that he should not do it.

To the two parasites on industry, capital and land, we have added a third parasite, "Trade Monopoly." Not enough that we are held up by those Claude Duvals of Political Economy, Rent and Interest, the state must now step in with paternal solicitude, and hand us over to the Dick Turpins of tariff protection.

And does protection encourage home industry? Not unless pampered indolence is a spur to effort, and helplessness leads to self support.

We have by tariff legislation artificially nurtured and rendered chronically helpless and dependent the industries of the nation. We have withdrawn them from the wholesome and invigorating effects of open competition, and exposed them to the baneful and unhealthy influence of State paternalism. With most unjust discrimination against self-respecting and self-supporting industries of our land and at their expense, we are maintaining a perpetual pension fund for industrial failures and incapables—a sort of public almshouse to prop up business incompetency.

The great stimulus to excellence is this very competition from which we are shielding our "protected" industries. Under its spur, ingenuity, skill and ability are brought into full play, which backed by manly self-reliance is the foundation of enduring success.

But we have done worse. Not only are we undermining industrial integrity and self-reliance, but the enervating influences of a pernicious state interference is invading our social life. Our meddlesome paternalism is breeding a race of moral weaklings, lacking the stamina of manhood and self-restraint. As physical and mental excellence and supremacy are the result of persistent effort to overcome obstacles and difficulties, so character and moral fibre are the result of a constant struggle to overcome temptation. And yet forsooth, we must discourage self-restraint and bring up a race coddled into an artificial state of respectability and rectitude by restrictive measures prompted by a narrow puritanical religious paternalism! We must be our brother's keeper lest he go wrong!

We are presumably a nation of freemen and pride ourselves on our free institutions, and yet our personal liberties are curtailed to a degree that would not be tolerated in any monarchy in Europe. We dare not trust ourselves lest freedom for good become a license for evil! Let us be men, and prove ourselves worthy of the blessings of liberty. Let us forever and without revocation annul all blue-laws and other laws restrictive of personal freedom and give character a chance. Let manhood and personal responsibility assert themselves, and we shall bring up men worthy of self government, a race of freemen, self-respecting, self-supporting and self-reliant.

Neither morality nor prosperity can be legislated into a nation, but they may be seriously hindered by restrictive laws. Family training and home influences determine the one and individual effort the other.

Let us not delude ourselves further in regard to state paternalism, for it spells "social slavery." Annul all trade limitations and abolish all restrictions. Let us have social and industrial freedom in the widest sense. Revoke all tariff duties, excises and other taxes, for they are not only restrictive of personal freedom, but they are violations of the rights of property. There is but one justifiable tax and that is the land tax—the "single tax" advocated by Mr. Henry George. This tax equalizes the benefits of land tenure and therein lies its warrant in justice.

What is the basis of material prosperity?

First, as explained, we must set right our perverted economic conditions. This will emancipate labor from monopoly dictation and make it non-competitive as far as opportunities of employment are concerned. If under such favorable conditions, we likewise make our labor effective, and prevent unnecessary wastes of effort, all the requirements for a rapid material advancement are satisfied.

At the head of all wastes of human effort is the appalling waste due to the maintenance of large standing armies and floating navies. Fortunately in this country the expenditures for military and naval establishments are not very great, though there is a dangerous tendency to increased appropriations for that purpose.

Corrupt political influences, however, competing for the vote of the veterans of the late war by promises of liberal party legislation has swelled the pension roll until by reckless and criminally extravagant appropriations the burthens of the people have been enormously increased. The lofty ideal of patriotic duty has been degraded and debased to the sordid level of party spoils, and an indiscriminate grant of pensions has resulted in a disgraceful scramble for State patronage, so that, to be enrolled on the pension list, no longer confers honor or distinction to the beneficiary, greatly to the disparagement of the truly deserving heroes of the war.

What we now pay in pensions alone will rival the outlays of some of the great European powers in the maintenance of large standing armies.

Justice must be the aim of Social Reform and our pension laws should be revised. The pension roll should be a roll of honor and merit.

Expenses for military and naval purposes must be kept in check.

The greatest waste of the country's wealth, not excepting even the waste due to standing armies, is the waste due to enforced idleness, which in the case of our present hard times, we tried to measure statistically. It must not be forgotten, however, that much enforced idleness prevails in the most prosperous times due to the monopoly influences we have traced. This waste under normal conditions, probably greatly exceeds the amount of our pension rolls. This enormous loss will be eliminated when we emancipate labor from these monopolies by our Money Reform.

The wastes due to Government extravagance through party corruption will cease when the "spoils" system is eradicated from politics. Social justice will improve the public morals, and constitutional limitations will prevent abuse of the public patronage.

Much effort is uselessly wasted in the production of unnecessary and injurious luxuries, such as alcoholic drinks, which not only imply a waste of wealth, but are a deteriorating influence on productive efficiency. However, reform here must be left to strengthening of character and moral responsibility, which will come from greater personal freedom and greater well-being.

The wastes of efficiency due to trade restrictions we have already noticed. These will cease when such restrictions are removed. The wastes of effort in the useless mining of gold and silver for money use will cease with the issue of the Reform Money.

Our system of industrial production and distribution of products is fortuitous and unscientific; and as a consequence very wasteful. The losses due to our competitive business methods are great; indeed the sums annually spent for profitless advertising and useless maintenance of an army of middlemen and agents to stimulate trade are enormous. The waste due to misdirected energy and misapplied effort in conducting production and exchange is appalling. But the process is improving. The system of industrial production and exchange by Trusts and Combinations is simply an improved method with the wasteful features of competition and fortuitous production eliminated. The Trust is a scientific method of industrial production and distribution, and should be encouraged. These combinations are beneficial where free trade and free competition prevail, but tariff restrictions make of them dangerous and unscrupulous monopolies. The trust is the germ of a great movement toward productive efficiency and must revolutionize our present wasteful methods. The output and distribution of all the industries of the world must sooner or later come under the control of organized intelligence, and the Trust is such an organized effort. It should be noticed, that the trend of industrial effort is constantly toward greater efficiency. Every invention, every labor saving device, every short cut to wealth production, every improvement which increases the efficiency of human labor is a blessing. It makes our houses better, our clothes better, our conveniences greater, and stimulates to greater industry and effort. We obtain more of the conveniences of life for less effort than before. These improved methods do not lessen employment—on the contrary they open up new opportunities. If our efficiency were a hundred times greater than now, the opportunities for employment would not be less, but more numerous, for with every new opportunity, new possibilities would be opened up. Work is infinite, and if the avenues to it are closed, it is our own fault.

There is another source of waste, which with economic justice and scientific management will vastly decrease and in time entirely disappear, providing the tendency to over-population can be kept in check. I refer to the physically, morally and mentally afflicted—the crippled, blind, insane and otherwise physically incapable; the drunkards and criminals and otherwise morally depraved; the indolent, incompetent, paupers and beggars—all of them wards of the State.

The pauper and criminal are to a great extent more sinned against than sinning. When we have first extirpated the great economic crime at the root of our social system—when civilization rhymes with equalization and not spoliation, then we may be able to deal successfully with the class for whose wrong-doing our social injustice is largely responsible. With one hand society robs the laborer of the means of subsistence and self support, and with the other punishes him for stealing bread to save his family from starvation. And this is justice! A social system based on injustice naturally breeds crime and moral depravity.

Our economic perversions are probably largely responsible for all social immorality and corruption, for they teach that wealth may be had without compensatory effort. They have converted us into a nation of financial speculators, stock gamblers and cunning schemers, all in a mad, reckless, frenzied rush for wealth—all expecting to get rich without honest work—rich and independent at some one's else expense. Honesty is a relative term. The ethics of social morality is largely a matter of method. There is method even in appropriation. The methods of house-breaker and thief are crude and unscientific beside the subtle refinements of economic absorption. The robber goes to jail for stealing a purse. He is disgraced and degraded. He suffers privations and indignities. But parasitic wealth, with its hand in every wage earner's pocket, dwells in a palace in luxurious ease and affluence, while an army of industrial slaves does its bidding and society goes down on its deferential knees to its kind. It is fondled, flattered, and eulogized. It is merely a difference in method.

We cannot expect pure water from a polluted source, any more than we may expect virtue from vice.

The moral diseases of mankind are, all of them, in their last analysis, traceable to abnormal social conditions present and past, and their cure must of necessity imply social reform. Chronic destitution leads to despair. Poverty is the margin where human endurance ends either in self-abasement and dependence, or asserts itself in self-destruction or crime. The unjust distribution of wealth, the affluence of the corrupt, and the success of the unscrupulous, all seem to proclaim the absence of social justice and fair play, and furnish the criminal what he believes to be a justification for his crime. We must therefore begin with society first before we apply our morality to those whom its sin helped to deprave.

We should invoke science in the treatment of vice and crime. Chronic cases of depravity should not be permitted to breed their kind. Vice should not be suppressed, but extirpated by scientific and humane methods. All criminals should be made self-supporting. Enforced idleness in our prisons is a crime against the prisoners and against society. It is a great waste of wealth and a tribute on honest labor. The position taken by trade organizations on the subject of prison labor is another instance of fallacious reasoning due to our wretched economic perversions. When it becomes clear, that under healthy economic conditions the opportunities for work will always overtake the labor seeking them and that employment and not labor is competitive, the short sighted policy in regard to prison labor will become quite apparent.

Then there is the army of the incompetents and incapables, from which pauperism is largely recruited. These are the stragglers, weaklings and social failures, bringing up the rear of the industrial procession who, in the race of life, are left to perish by the wayside. The requirements of race superiority imply under the cruel operation of nature's law the destruction of the weak. To foster disease and inferiority by protective methods is to encourage race deterioration, therefore all congenital cases of general worthlessness must not be permitted to perpetuate their kind. By the wise enforcement of humane methods of prevention, chronic, physical and moral worthlessness will gradually disappear and cease to be a burthen on the rest of mankind.

Another source of waste is the enforced idleness due to labor strikes and lockouts. These are the protests of oppressed labor against unjust economic conditions, which make it competitive and place it at the mercy of monopoly.

The avenues of employment are closed by the tollgates of monopoly, and helpless labor stands without, asking permission to earn a living. The toll is the price labor pays for the privilege of earning, and only those who can pay the price pass through.

Labor hopelessly competitive has no redress but that which may come from organization for the common defense, and concerted action. The strike is a protest against industrial injustice.

Under normal conditions labor will be free and non-competitive. Wages and services will be reciprocal; laborer and employer will meet on equal terms, both earning their income by productive services, neither having any advantages over the other, except in brains and efficiency, each rewarded according to his industrial ability.

Under such conditions Trades Unions and other Labor Organizations will have no grievances, and no enemy, and will resolve themselves into societies for social and intellectual advancement.

With all these great wastes of human effort eliminated, the productive efficiency will be largely enhanced. The increased well-being of the depleted millions, will tend to their elevation and refinement, and conduce to still greater efficiency.

It must not be imagined that we have reached the zenith of industrial advancement. We are still only at the beginning and evolution is slow and painful. The vicissitudes of industrial progress are great and throw out of employment temporarily, specialized labor, through pressure of constant changes in methods and improvements. It should be a fixed State policy to lessen waste through temporary idleness of such as are stranded in industrial centers through the exigencies of trade.

The land tax will yield revenue far beyond purely State uses and the surplus must be applied to public improvements. Work on public improvements should always be on tap to anyone passing the requisite test of efficiency. There should be a lowest rate of pay for a certain recognized class of work and this pay should not be so large as to be an inducement to seek public work in preference to private enterprise, but to relieve honest and efficient effort fairly. Promotions to higher grades of work could be made from this class. The Public Improvement Bureau would then always be a guarantee of employment to the efficient and prove a national boon, as establishing a labor overflow outlet, and a lowest level of comfort below which competent labor could never fall. The different Bureau districts should be competitive with one another as to comparative showings of expenses for paving and excavating, etc., to insure greater efficiency for money expended.

A surplus fund for Public Improvements should always be kept on hand to meet industrial and other emergencies. Droughts, floods, local disasters and other derangements temporarily throw workers out of employment and debar them from earning a living. Public improvement work is an asylum for such as cannot at once accommodate themselves to new conditions, welcoming them to earn an honest living instead of depending on charity. Public improvements add to the nation's wealth and benefit the community to the full value of the money expended; why then allow any waste of human effort? Enforced idleness is a public loss and a great hardship to the unemployed. To be out of work means not to earn; not to earn means not to spend, and therefore, not to consume; lessened consumption means lessened production, and this means hardship to other producers, so that one part of the community cannot be affected without affecting the well-being of the whole. Here, therefore, comes in the legitimate function of the State. The individual can look after his own affairs better than the State, but the State can look after the collective welfare better than the individual. Of course, if relief measures could be assured by private enterprise, by some method of insurance, it might be a preferable method, as self-help is the best help, but in the absence of such some public provision must be made for lessening the evils of temporary idleness.

The money volume being ample, the surplus fund may be allowed to accumulate without prejudice to commerce and industry.

Reckless extravagance of government must be checked. One of the reasons of corruption and jobbery is that no efficient system of competitive checks on public expense and work output have been introduced. All government work must be competitive as to expense and efficiency, and "comparison statements" should be instituted as a test gauge of public service. The comparison blanks should be designed on a per capita or some other convenient basis of comparison, and should show items of expense of the past year as compared with expenses of some prior year of greatest economy. The heads of departments should be held responsible for expenses, and subject to removal for lack of economy. In this way only can we expect efficiency in public service. There are several industrial branches where collective effort would be more efficient and beneficial than private enterprise, if political corruption could be eliminated. Public management of the post office has been a source of great convenience and saving. In like manner, but to a vastly greater degree, the public management of money and banking will be a boon. In a minor though very important degree, the collective management of the telegraph and public highways would be a blessing. The telegraph, railroads and canals are national industrial opportunities, and the benefits of same should be equalized. Franchises should not be granted to private individuals, and highways should not be permitted to fall under the control of any individual or corporation. But unless we divorce the public business from party corruption and pillage, we are probably better off to entrust as little business to Government as possible. That under proper checks these public enterprises can be successfully carried on and economically managed, there is absolutely no doubt, but such efficiency implies constitutional reforms, limiting political interferences in the people's business and establishing the public service on a scientific basis. Then and only then may we expect honesty in office. Most of our public and private corruption is due to the immorality underlying our civilization. When social justice has been inaugurated we may expect a very material change in public morals.

Public outlays must be jealously watched and administrations must be judged by standards of public economy.

Extravagance leads to corruption and to national decadence. However, all immoral tendencies will be more or less checked when the efficient and strong are taxed exactly in proportion to their land holdings, and are obliged to pay these taxes out of the proceeds of honest effort and not out of the sweat of other men's labor. The same men, who with criminal recklessness, voted away extravagant appropriations of the people's money under the spoils system, will now begin to consider their own pockets into which the tribute of despoiled labor will have ceased to flow.

If our present imperfect civil service system is inadequate to give us an honest administration of public affairs, we must so alter it that partisan interference can affect civil service only on lines of greater efficiency and economy.

No social reform can be complete which does not provide for the nationalization of public monopolies. While we fully realise the corruptions and short comings of public service, we are forced to admit one of two things or both of them; either the corruptions of public office and inefficiency of public service are due to some inherent wrong in our system which may be removed, or we are incapable of self-government. There seems to be no doubt as to the true cause of misgovernment. With the advent of social justice, new social conditions, and political regeneration must logically follow. Under such conditions the corrupt dispensation of public patronage, the granting of trade monopolies, the lobbying of franchises and privileges, and the general legislative catering to private greed and selfishness, cannot continue very long. Political corruption and depravity must in a large measure cease when class legislation and paternalism are prohibited, and when partisan interference in public business is checked.

Under improved social conditions, and proper civil service regulations, we may expect efficient service and economy in public affairs.

The highways belong to the people and it seems like a great privilege that any one person or corporation should monopolize a public convenience. Railroads, roadways, waterways and telegraphs must ultimately come under the management of the people, and though immediate change from private control may be undesirable, such nationalization should be kept constantly in view. The "land purchase act" should cover the purchase of all the improvements and equipments of such of the public monopolies as it may be deemed expedient to nationalize.

In the managements of the railroads, telegraphs and the post office, and in the control of land and money, the State function is not only legitimate and proper, but urgent. These are public interests and not private concerns.

But the commerce and industries are essentially private affairs and should be left to regulate themselves. We should not only resent any approach to State interference with trade, but even insist upon the annulment of the constitutional clause which empowers congress "to regulate commerce with foreign nations and among the several States," seeing what injury has been done by the injudicious exercise of this power. Under no pretext whatever should congress be permitted to place restrictions on trade.

Both in the regulation and management of the commerce and the industries we are justified in warning the State, "Hands off."

CHAPTER VIII.

In a Society based on injustice the "survival of the fittest" means the survival of the unscrupulous.

There can be no honor in wealth acquired under unjust conditions. Do we not all of us feel that somehow the millionaires could not possibly have earned a tithe of their vast fortunes?

Let us for a moment contemplate Mr. Thos. G. Shearman's classification of some of the millionaires of eight years ago which he used in his estimates of wealth distribution. The figures are taken from the New York World of June 20th, 1897. While the estimates may now be wide of the mark in some cases, in a general way they will answer our purpose.

J. J. Astor.	150 millions.
C. Vanderbilt.	100 "
W. K. Vanderbilt.	100 "
Jay Gould.	100 "
Leland Stanford.	100 "
J. D. Rockefeller.	100 "
Estate of A. Packer.	70 "
John I. Blair.	60 "
Estate of Chas. Croker.	60 "
William Astor.	50 "
W. W. Astor.	50 "

Russell Sage,   -   -   -   50   "
E. A. Stevens,   -   -   50   "
Etc., etc., etc.

Referring back to our definition of money we found it to be simply a receipt for services rendered—a voucher for work done usefully and productively—which empowered the holder to levy on Society for an equivalent either in present services, or in past services as represented in commodities.

If we come honestly by this money it must represent something we have done productively for the comfort or advancement of our fellow men upon whom we levy for an equivalent. In other words, the money must come to us as a reward for useful effort.

How much of this wealth represents actual services rendered mankind by the possessors of it? Are these men intellectual or industrial giants, possessing prodigious powers of production and conferring on society vast benefits? If not, how did they come by this money? If these millions do not represent the productive effort of the millionaires possessing them whose productive effort can they represent? Plainly speaking, how much of this wealth is of parasitic growth and how much honest flesh and blood, and where in justice should the knife of confiscation be applied? Let us see. What is a million dollars? The average yearly reward of human effort in the

United States is about six hundred dollars per year per worker. If by excellent management and great self-denial half of the sum be saved yearly, it would take three thousand three hundred and thirty-three years of continuous work and abstinence to save one million of dollars. That is, if a man of average ability commenced saving up half of his earnings about the time of the exodus of the Israelites, he would by this time have accumulated about one million dollars; and yet some of these people are able to draw an income of from six to nine millions a year!

If, after the ground had been cursed for his sake, and he was condemned to eat bread in the sweat of his face, Adam had thought best to invest in a Life Insurance policy maturing A. D. 1897, and had saved half the earnings of a man of average ability, his total deposits up to date would amount to only about 1,800,000 dollars. And yet we have men reputed to be possessed of something like one hundred times that amount of wealth! Surely the earth brings forth no thorns and thistles for these men, nor do they eat their bread in the sweat of their brow. How did they get it? Will Mr. Astor claim that he or his ancestors have actually rendered to society in services an equivalent of his enormous possessions? Will he claim, honor bright, that his useful efforts to human kind equalled the productive work of say five men of average ability? Will the natural modesty of Mr. Vanderbilt permit him to claim that he has conferred on his fellowmen services worth the efforts of say ten men of average ability? Perhaps the author is not very appreciative, but he really doubts if some of our millionaires could earn an honest living if left to their own resources. And as to those capable of self support, has not the leisure of Labor's competence been sacrificed to give them training and education? Whence came these millions and whose money are they? They surely represent the sweat of good honest toil and effort. Whose toil is it? The people's. These millions are almost wholly the tribute exacted from human effort for the use of the artificial monopoly, money, and the natural monopoly, land. Interest on "Capital" and rent on land and speculation in these monopolies have been chiefly the sources of these fortunes. They represent the drain on human industry by the idle and unjust possession of the people's natural productive opportunities.

It is not here contended that there are not men capable of earning great wealth. On the contrary, there are thousands of intellectual and industrial giants and leaders of industrial effort who have conferred great benefits on society. It is difficult to see, for instance, how millions could pay an Edison for the benefits he has conferred on mankind. There is no doubt whatever that many of our very wealthy men have by real ability and efficiency conferred on society certain substantial benefits, but as a rule the rewards are out of all proportion to the services. An honest social condition based on fair play, will give all men their deserved reward, and wealth under such a condition will be a true criterion of "worth" and a certificate of honor. It is quite probable that many of the competent rich, who have conferred benefits on society, would be glad if the parasitic features of wealth did not exist, as there can be no honor in wealth acquired without compensatory effort.

We have spoken of equity in the liquidation of the claims of present land holders. In the face of the great injustice to the expatriated and dispossessed, would it really be justice to those whom present social conditions have so grievously wronged, that on top of other private fortunes of these unjustly rich, the State should cash their holdings in full? It would seem to be a great perversion of justice to do it. The State ought to set a price limit to land tenure, beyond which, compensation should not, in justice to the common interest, be permitted. The land in excess of such holdings should revert to the national domain.

Abstract justice can not of course be done; the iniquities of our social conditions have caused irreparable suffering to the despoiled. Out of the privations and sufferings of the wronged, the unjustly rich have for centuries enjoyed especial comforts and advantages, and neither the sufferings of the despoiled, nor the pleasures and privileges of the benefited can be revoked. The past lies beyond the reach of justice. The present may however be remedied, though at best the reorganization on lines of justice must largely partake of relative ethics. The aim should be, the greatest justice to the greatest number, seeking the even justice of all.

But while the injustice of full liquidation of the claims of the immensely rich is quite apparent, can we consistently and within the scope of constitutional rights establish an arbitrary limit of land compensation, and will not such distinction in land claims work hardship as between those rich in land, and those rich in other properties? At best, ethically speaking, social re-organization is full of difficulties. Our aim should be first, to establish just economic conditions and relieve the socially wronged from further spoliation; if then some of the wealth acquired under unjust social conditions can be recovered to the people, it certainly seems right that an effort should be made to do so.

The people are greater than constitutions, and whether liquidation to the full value or within prescribed limits be agreed upon, will wholly depend upon the interpretation of the word "Justice."

There is no doubt, however, that pending reorganization and readjustment on reform lines, which must be a very slow process, self-interest will in the meanwhile so operate, as to defeat any government scheme seeking to appropriate any part of the vast estates of the unjustly rich to public use. We will thereby be spared any ethical qualms of conscience on the score of possible injustice being done to the parasitic minority.

Were it, however, practicable to restore to the people some of this unjustly acquired wealth, and the limit of land ownership subject to compensation were fixed at, say, the average wealth of the nation per family, which is about five thousand dollars, it is fair to estimate that more than ninty-eight per cent. of the population would have their land claims liquidated in full and that less than two per cent. would be affected by such compensation limit. The immensely and unjustly rich would still possess an enormous advantage over the masses by virtue of their vast industrial and commercial investments, but no one would begrudge them these advantages, if further drain on the people's resources might be stopped.

It is fair to estimate the value of the land reverting to the national domain by virtue of such a compensation limit, as exceeding ten billions of dollars. Reform money to the full value of this land might be issued and held in the public treasury as a reserve fund. From this reserve fund our nine different kinds of money and obligations could be redeemed. There is no doubt that the demonetization of gold by the United States will at once depreciate its value and the nation will lose the difference between its money value and its metal value. What the loss will be on silver bullion we are in a fair position to estimate: the depreciation on gold will be fully as much. Our loss on coin and bullion will probably reach the neighborhood of 800 millions of dollars or more. This together with our irredeemable paper will deplete the new treasury of something like 1150 millions of Reform Dollars, but it will be cheap riddance of bad rubbish to forever retire our absurd coin and paper money.

To briefly recapitulate:—We inferred deductively that an ideal system of society would be such, that while conceding to the individual the greatest possible personal freedom consistent with the highest welfare of society as a whole, it would guarantee to every member of the community an equal chance in the race of life without prejudice—an equal opportunity without favor or hindrance. That if we enter the arena of life on equal terms as regards the industrial opportunities, then all the requirements of social ethics will be satisfied.

Does our present system fulfill the requirements of such an ideal? Are the conditions such as to guarantee fair play to every one in the struggle for subsistence? Our investigations can leave no room for doubt or hesitation, and we declare most conclusively and emphatically, No. The conditions are unfair and unjust. At the base of society we find a grievous wrong—at the core of civilization a social crime. Two great industrial opportunities of productive effort, the benefits of which should be common, have been left to the sport of private speculation and monopoly. The shrewd and cunning obtain control of these opportunities, monopolize the avenues of employment and thus hold the key to the industrial situation. The restrictions which tribute puts upon industry, render labor hopelessly competitive and place industrial effort completely at the mercy of idle possession. Labor is degraded and enslaved; pauperism, crime and immorality are encouraged. A small minority absorb the nation's productive output and live in luxurious ease and idleness at the expense of depleted millions. This in short is the present social condition. The evils have been known for centuries, but the causes were not traced to the perversions of Political Economy. All social reformers have keenly felt the injustice of these conditions and have suggested measures of relief, but these schemes of reform, if not simply ameliorative and superficial expedients, were subversive of a natural order of social evolution. Nearly all of them imply legislative acts and forms restrictive of personal freedom, and obstructive of natural and healthy progress and development. No social reform can ever become practical or successful which does not rest on natural laws, and which has to be propped up by artificial legal contrivances to make it operative. Such a system implies coercion and can mean but one thing—social despotism. No social reform can be lasting which does not guarantee to every individual that greatest of all boons—freedom. We must be free; socially free, industrially free, politically free—free to move and have our being without "paternal" restraints.

The money reform here outlined contemplates no abridgment of personal freedom. It implies no social restrictions, beyond those absolutely necessary to maintain national coherence and integrity and those social safeguards which prevent men from injuring one another not only socially and physically, but also industrially. It guarantees even justice to every man and rewards exertion in the exact ratio of useful effort. The individual who renders human kind the highest service obtains the highest rewards, but these rewards do not empower him to enslave his less favored brother, or levy tribute on the sweat and toil of other men. His superior abilities do not permit him to take undue advantage of his fellowman.

Emancipate Land and render Capital premiumless, and social reform is an accomplished fact, without the sacrifice of the only thing worth living for in this world—personal freedom. The much abused sentiment "Liberty, Equality and Fraternity" will then for the first time be more than an empty phrase, and the grand word "Democracy," as an embodiment of equality, will acquire a meaning it never had before. Plutocracy and aristocracy, the offspring of parasitic wealth, will be things of the past.

How much will the "Money Reform" system save to the nation?

On the basis of Mr. Shearman's estimates, more than 76 per cent. of the nation's wealth is in the hands of less than three per cent. of the people. As the forces of wealth concentration have not ceased operating since Mr. Shearman published his figures over eight years ago, it is presumable that the disparities have not, since that time, grown less, but rather more intensified.

It is quite fair to estimate that about 70 of the 76 per cent. of the wealth in the hands of the parasitic "three per cent." is interest bearing, and that probably 10 of the remaining 24 per cent. is involved in one way or another in indebtedness and also yields rent or interest. Thus four fifths of the capital of the United States would be yielding "income." To be quite within reason we will assume that only three-quarters of the nation's capital yields such revenue. If, on the basis of the Eleventh Census $62,600,000,000 out of the $65,000.000,000 be the value of private wealth in 1890, then the capital on which interest was paid will foot up about $46,950,000,000.

All conveniences conducive to shelter and comfort; all improvements and facilities aiding industrial effort; all methods, appliances and machinery may be classed as the tools of production. They are man's equipment, and land is his workshop. More than three-quarters of the workshop and the tools of industrial production are in the hands of the parasitic "three." Perverted economic conditions have made it possible for an insignificant minority to obtain control of this vast wealth and to use it with despotic power for the indefinite and continued exploitation and enslavement of the helpless wealth producers. It is a system of economic plunder for which the term "social infamy" is a mild expression.

The prevailing bank rate on "gilt edge" security is six per cent. All capital therefore assumes as its right a toll of six per cent. in addition to the costs of its maintenance and superintendence. The whole of this 46950 millions of dollars worth of property, in addition to the price of its maintenance, therefore claims a toll of six per cent. for hire. We have assumed that if the collective people undertook banking, the actual cost of banking services would probally fall below the half of one per cent. Let us assume this excessive rate of the half of one per cent. as covering the cost of banking. Then such percentage will constitute a legitimate charge for services, and all capital will claim a right to collect for such services in addition to charges for cost of maintenance and services connected with its renting. While now we are paying six per cent. interest for capital's hire, we would under the new conditions pay only this "bank service" charge of the half of one per cent. The five and a half per cent. additional we are now paying thus appears to be a tribute to idle possession, and in excess of any productive service. Five and a half per cent.

on 46,950 millions of dollars per year is 2,582 millions of dollars, which amount goes to build up an aristocracy of wealth, and for which society receives no equivalent. Let us see what this sum of money means. Remember that these estimates apply to the year 1890, and that since then the nation's wealth has very largely increased, and the conditions for the depleted majority are probably more unfavorable.

On the basis of the population for 1890 and our estimate, every family in the land is paying these social parasites, on an average, over two hundred dollars per year! On the basis of Mr. Waldron's estimate of yearly productive efficiency this tribute to parasitic wealth corresponds to nearly twenty per cent. of the average yearly income! In other words, our economic perversions have taken twenty per cent. from the gross earnings of labor and put the money into the pockets of an idle aristocracy! These are amazing figures and it behooves us to thoroughly understand how they are obtained. Let us measure this economic drain on human effort by a more direct method.

The country's total wealth value at this moment will probably not fall short of 80 billions of dollars, while the annual industrial output may be safely estimated at about 16 billions of dollars. Thus for every

5 dollars' worth of wealth. there is a dollar's worth of productive output per year. About three-quarters of this 5 dollars' worth of wealth may be considered as interest bearing capital, so that it takes $3.75 in capital to yield productively 1 dollar's worth of new wealth per year. For the repairs and maintenance of this capital it will cost on an average about 4 per cent., and for bank service charge about ½ per cent., making a legitimate charge of 4 1-2 per cent. on $3.75, or nearly 17 cents. This amount must be deducted from the gross productive output of 1 dollar to obtain labor's just earnings. But over and above this legitimate charge, there remains a tribute of 5½ per cent premium for which there is no service equivalent to society. This premium amounts to about twenty cents on the gross productive output of one dollar. Deducting the 17 cents for maintenance and for services, we obtain 83 cents as the legitimate income of labor. Upon every 83 cents which labor earns, this premium charge of 20 cents falls as a tribute, or in other words, on every dollar of labor's just earnings, capital levies a toll of 24 per cent!

In these estimates no account is taken of the volume of paper money in circulation, nor the value of products in process of consumption on which interest is being paid, which would tend to swell the economic drain on labor's income.

But this is not all. Something like twenty-eight per cent of the millionaires owe their wealth to protected industries. The tariff tax on necessities, by shifting the burthen of taxation on the ninety-five per cent socially wronged, relieves parasitic wealth from just assessment, thus again favoring its growth. The enhanced cost of living to the despoiled ninety-five per cent., from which tariff monopoly wrings its millions, further reduces their earnings. We may safely say that through enhanced cost of living alone the infamous tariff tax probably takes ten per cent. more out of the pockets of the unfortunate worker. Thus the worker's tribute to the monopoly of opportunities is about thirty three per cent. of his actual earnings. an average of about three hundred dollars per family for the creation and maintenance of an idle proprietary class! Thus a sum much larger than the cost of the civil war, is diverted annually from the pockets of the people and goes to swell the redundance of the "parasitic" rich.

For about five years during and after the civil war, a period of unexampled prosperity prevailed owing to the release yearly into industrial channels of some five or six hundred millions of dollars. When through jobbery and economic plunder these millions found their way back again to the coffers of the rich, and the people assumed the liquidation of the debt at rates which more than doubled the principal, industrial activity ceased and prosperity came to an end.

If setting free such an amount of money per year under a system of economic spoliation caused so much prosperity, what may we not expect under a system of social justice, when something like four times that amount of money per capita remains annually in the hands of the people for circulation in trade channels? It might appear to the reader that the words "Industrial Enslavement" and "Industrial Independence" are mere figures of speech. Far from it. On the basis of the census of 1890 there were 12,690,151 families in the land. If our estimates of labor's tribute to idle possession are correct, then more than four million families were exclusively devoted to the maintenance in idle luxury of less than four hundred thousand parasitic families! Is this not industrial slavery? It is worse in a way than actual slave ownership, for here, starvation is the whip of compulsion, and the slave owners are spared the bother and inconvenience of taking care of their human chattels. Our Political Economy does that, and assumes the moral responsibility too. Is there any wonder that we are rushing headlong to national self-destruction? The greater the wealth output, the heavier the tribute and more hopeless the bondage. The economic blackmail not only depletes the workers but prevents them from earning, by putting a toll on opportunity. Better abandon civilization and go back to primitive methods than submit to this social loot. Better any form of socialistic despotism, than such iniquity. Better the dead level of a joyless and depressing communism than a civilization based on injustice.

Establish Money Reform and Industrial bondage is at an end. The idle rich will cease to thrive and the money power will be broken. The chronically idle will be profitably employed; the vagrant, tramp and criminal, will now join the industrial army in an honest effort to earn a living, and become self-supporting. With fully employed labor, with increased productive efficiency, and with the establishment of social justice, what degree of advancement may we not expect?

That these economic wrongs should have been borne in silence these many years, might show how long human nature may be imposed upon before being provoked to overt acts of social revolt. But forbearance is not one of the virtues of the slumbering giant, and it is to be hoped that social reform will overtake his awakening to the true realization of his wrongs, or the earth may tremble with his wrath and fury.

The provocation has been great and the injustice monstrous, and were it not that familiarity with misery breeds indifference to it, and that we grow callous to suffering, the social iniquities would seem to be past endurance

But nature is not without a parallel strongly suggestive of our social perversions of justice, and the comparison is not without its lessons.

The ichneumon fly is parasitic in the living bodies of caterpillars and the larvae of other insects. With cruel cunning and ingenuity surpassed only by man, this depraved and unprincipled insect perforates the struggling caterpillar, and deposits her eggs in the living, writhing body of her victim. Eruptions appear on the surface of the unfortunate worm, and in due course of time the atrocious brood is hatched. With the refinement of innate cruelty, these parasites eat their way into the living substance of their unwilling but helpless host, avoiding all the vital parts to prolong the agony of a lingering death. The worm is their "capital" and they are taking their "income." They are consuming the "interest" and "saving" up the "principal." The toil and suffering of saving is entirely vicarious—the worm does that. We might, did we possess the eloquence of a Bastiat, go into ecstacies over the glorious "harmonies" of nature's economic methods! But what about the worm? Nature's malevolence may be beneficial to man, but how about the worm? Is there no redress for the poor worm? No; he must bear the invasion with good grace, for should he presume to complain about the social "harmonies", the "parasites" would straightway turn upon him and denounce him as an "agitator"—perhaps call him a "socialist" or some other disagreeable name. And as to the eviction of these unwelcome tenants, who could be so shockingly heartless as to propose such an outrageous measure! The presumption! Is it not their inheritance, and have they not the right of possession?

Such appear to be the arguments of the parasitically rich and of their parasitic supporters.

People of America! Will you tolerate this state of things any longer? Will you see the continued perpetration of a great social wrong and remain the passive victims of it? Delays are dangerous, the power of aggregated wealth grows apace and is becoming more aggressive as it grows stronger. Further degradation and enslavement of the masses can be the only outcome.

Even now strong repressive measures are invoked to keep down social uprisings and discontent. Only "strong" governments can successfully maintain "order" in a society where Labor is forcibily "held up" and fleeced by its refined economic methods.

Already the staunch supporters of Monarchy, tauntingly point, in vindication of "strong government" theories, to our social and political corruptions, and watch with secret joy the forces of disintegration which are slowly but surely hastening our downfall.

The menace to our liberties is this unjust wealth accumulation. No republic can long withstand the subtle influence of a corrupt plutocracy. This wealth rightfully belongs to the people and its unjust appropriation is a usurpation of power which must logically lead to despotism and ultimate national decadence. Other great nations have succumbed to these very influences, and from the sepulchres of the past, their buried civilizations appeal to us in mute eloquence, and bid us beware of their untimely fate. But we have our warnings. Already the rights of free speech and protests of labor have been judicially assailed. Even now over-zealous partisans of strong government measures, would lead to overt acts of oppression and repression, and an unscrupulous and mendacious press has voiced the sentiments. Thousand and one silent influences are at work slowly and imperceptably leading to greater arrogation of power by the rich and to the gradual abridgment of the people's liberties.

Shall we stem the tide that is bearing us on to national destruction? Let every man who has the welfare of mankind at heart, who loves his country and values liberty—who believes in justice and fair play, and desires a peaceful solution of our social woes, put his heart and soul into the cause of righting these iniquities. Let him assume the sacred duties of citizenship and vote for a reform.

The money power is formidable—vested rights and interests are powerful. The social parasites will be up in arms and fight for their very life, for all the "incomes" of the rich are menaced. All institutions which idly thrive at the expense of industry will be arrayed against us; even churches and "endowed" colleges depending on "annuities" have common interests with parasitic capital. A powerful press in the service of present interests will wage war to the death.

Shall we crush the money power or shall it crush us? We must face the foes of social justice at the polls in overwhelming numbers and forever efface the crime of centuries! Over ninety-five per cent. of the people are wronged by existing conditions and nothing but apathy and political indifference will put off reform so long deferred.

The principles we have enunciated may be condensed into a political creed as follows:

1. Land emancipation by purchase; present holders of land to receive certificates to the full appraised value of their holdings. The nationalization by purchase, of railroads, waterways and telegraphs by the issue of similar certificates.

The Government of the United States to declare these certificates to be the lawful and constitutional money of the nation.

3. The value of the money to be regulated by the land tax rate on a uniform per capita assessment basis.

4. The volume of the money to be maintained on a uniform per capita basis and to be of such amplitude as to make it premiumless.

Gold and other money-metals to be demonetized. All coin money and paper obligations to be redeemed into lawful money.

6. The organization of national Mercantile and Savings banks, and the establishment of a bank service charge.

7. The repeal of all tariffs, excise and internal revenue laws and all other taxes and the substitution therefor of the land tax.

8. Maintenance of a public improvement fund. The establishment of a perpetual employment opportunity for overflow labor seeking occupation, and the fixing of a lowest standard rate of pay for labor passing a certain prescribed test of fitness.

9. The passing of such constitutional measures or amendments as will place all public service out of

the reach of partisan influence or interference on any pretext but that of greater efficiency and economy of service.

10. Selective immigration.

Shall we proceed at once to organize the forces of reform, or shall we temporize and wait until the miseries of another industrial and business collapse drive the socially wronged to desperation and revolt?

We are now entering upon a period of so-called "prosperity." The monopoly guarded opportunities are once more opening up to anxious and expectant labor, starved into unconditional submission by enforced idleness. For the privilege of this "prosperity" labor will continue to pay the usual 33 per cent. commission to capital and the tariff monopolies, but it will gladly pay the tribute, if only permitted to earn.

Were an attempt made to openly rob labor of 33 per cent. of its earnings on some economical pretext, the people would immediately rise in their might and crush the taxing power out of existence, but by the subtle and insidious methods of economic absorption, parasitic wealth takes its toll out of labor's earnings before the worker's pay is considered, and so the stealage is not even suspected.

Can we bring the people to a realization of these great wrongs?

Between the apprehension of a social wrong and the tardy righting of it, there are for the reformer, many stages of bitter disappointment, vexation and trial. The obstacles are many, the inertia to change great, and the resistance obstinate. Look what it cost to break the chains of chattel slavery in this country! Will the emancipation of the industrial slave be as stubbornly contested? Yes, we may expect opposition which for rancour and malevolence will find no parallel in history. The rotten foundations of a thoroughly corrupt and dishonest civilization are threatened. The props of privilege and despotism are menaced. We must prepare for a long and desperate struggle with a powerful and unscrupulous foe. Fortunately there need be no violence. The social dry-rot and political corruption have not yet deprived us of our franchise; we may organize and vote, and if we suffer social injustice to continue, it will be our own fault.

The appeal goes forth to ministers of religion in the name of morality and righteousness—to journalists, publicists and writers in the name of justice and fairplay—to all men in the name of humanity, to join in the righting of these wrongs.

The appeal goes forth to every political sect and social reform party without distinction of creed—to every industrial and trade organization of whatever following, to sink their differences and successfully unite for the common good on the lines and principles herein set forth. Heretofore the social forces have been more or less at variance and working at cross-purposes for want of a definite economic principle on which all could unite and agree. That principle has now been proclaimed and a definite policy formulated. The opportune moment for concerted action is at hand. Let all unite in one grand protest against the iniquities of the present social maladjustments and forever crush the money power.

If the movement have in it the inspiration of truth and justice, it will sweep the country like a mighty tidal wave and carry everything before it. The time is ripe and the goal is in sight, but we need men, we need leaders, we need organization. Who will lead us out of the Industrial Bondage?

Workers: Industrial deliverance and social elevation are within your reach. You have the power, if you but use it, to be the masters of your own destinies.

Unite! Organize! Vote!

FINIS.

www.ingramcontent.com/pod-product-compliance
Lightning Source LLC
Chambersburg PA
CBHW020259170426
43202CB00008B/438